Psychopath

Understand the Mind of a Psychopathic Person

(How to Survive Relationships With Narcissists and Psychopaths)

Adam Utecht

Published By **Ryan Princeton**

Adam Utecht

Psychopath: Understand the Mind of a Psychopathic Person (How to Survive Relationships With Narcissists and Psychopaths)

ISBN   978-1-998901-90-6

No part of this guidbook shall be reproduced in any form without permission in writing from the publisher except in the case of brief quotations embodied in critical articles or reviews.

Legal & Disclaimer

The information contained in this book is not designed to replace or take the place of any form of medicine or professional medical advice. The information in this book has been provided for educational & entertainment purposes only.

The information contained in this book has been compiled from sources deemed reliable, and it is accurate to the best of the Author's knowledge; however, the Author cannot guarantee its accuracy and validity and cannot be held liable for any errors or omissions. Changes are periodically made to this book. You must consult your doctor or get professional medical advice before using any of the suggested remedies, techniques, or information in this book.

Table Of Contents

Chapter 1: Psychopath Definition and Victimization Plot...................................... 1

Chapter 2: CAB: Cognitive, Affective, and Behavior... 9

Chapter 3: In Depth Cognitive Traits 16

Chapter 4: Affective Traits 25

Chapter 5: Behavioral Traits................... 35

Chapter 6: Relationship Flags................. 46

Chapter 7: Secret Manipulation 55

Chapter 8: Sense of Freedom................. 64

Chapter 9: Concluding Thoughts: Seeking Help for You 68

Chapter 1: Psychopath Definition and Victimization Plot

Psychopaths may be lady or male. In cutting-edge years there is clinical evidence to reveal that psychopaths are born, not raised which offers the distinction among psychopaths and sociopaths. Studies show there may be a genetic trait inside the thoughts that proves a psychopath is born in choice to becoming mentally ill at a exceptional issue in lifestyles. There are 20 dispositions psychologist Dr. Hare created and revised over the years. These dispositions are commonly what the psychology international makes use of to determine if a person has psychopathic inclinations. It is likewise viable to have mind scans run of the suspected psychopath to decide inside the event that they've the neurobiological trait, which has been located over the last

30 years to be the not unusual issue in psychopathic behavior.

It must be stated that irrespective of the truth that the genetic issue is gift it does no longer recommend the character will become a very violent psychopath. There are masses of people which may be callous, lack compassion or love that have not given into their violent nature. They frequently come off coldhearted and without shame or remorse, however it does not propose they have risen to the extent of committing a crime or becoming a serial killer.

Nature Versus Nurture Debate

The argument in psychology has normally been nature in region of nurture. If a person is properly nurtured with love and a extremely good domestic, the concept is the individual ought to have a exceptional, stable lifestyles with a good deal less functionality to have a intellectual contamination or turn violent. The contrary issue of this is an unstable domestic life, in which abuse is not unusual and could deliver upward thrust to violence and likely flip a predisposed individual like a psychopath right into a killer. The surroundings, nature, way of life, and effect of others are in massive element perception to sculpt the ethical or unethical behavior of someone. While within the beginning it changed into a high-quality argument wherein to base psychology on, there is also loads of evidence to really display a psychopath raised in a great domestic can though come to be a violent killer.

Psychodynamic Diagnostic Manual Description

Before speaking about the victimization plot, one need to apprehend that psychopaths generally fall into one in every of businesses: passive or aggressive. Parasitic or passive psychopaths are usually based, not as aggressive, and tend to be a "non-violent manipulator." Henderson, a famend Nineteen Thirties psychologist, referred to as this kind the "con artist." Henderson furthermore said the aggressive psychopath is explosive and really predatory, typically a violent perpetrator. It is the aggressive type that one need to worry approximately the most due to the reality they're in a role to show into serial killers.

Victimizing for the Game of It All

The psychopath has a victimization plot, a purpose if you may, to harm others. An abusive psychopath harms others for the game. A exercising is prepared to be accomplished in keeping with the plot the psychopath determines, and ultimately, this character will typically win through doing harm to others. The damage inflicted can be religious, mental or bodily. It can also be monetary. Psychopaths normally will be inclined to art work on self-gratification, in which they want to control and function strength over others. Their want for cash, sex, status, and every now and then the illusion of marriage is immoderate.

Psychopaths are liars who placed on "the masks of sanity." This mask is something you could have hassle seeing via, without a doubt as everybody else throughout the psychopath. Your instinct would possibly show you chance is upon you, but the psychopath will make sure that is disarmed nearly the minute you begin to feel uncomfortable so that you can preserve hiding. One very important lesson about what defines a psychopath is they're especially smart. This intelligence permits them to be charismatic, foxy, and an "intra-species predator" as Dr. Hare stated in his e-book Without Conscience.

During the victimization plot, a psychopath can be regular and fine in a loving dating. They do that a fantastic way to assemble an exquisite reputation that covers up their last reason. The psychopath can surely turn others in competition to the individual being harmed as a way to have more a laugh. The community will regularly maintain in thoughts and revel in being with the psychopath, even when someone is already beginning to figure out they're a psychopath. They can examine others like a ebook, becoming the very component as a way to have them desired whilst others are stressing.

The purpose varies. Psychopaths may also look for a person who's lonely or has severa strain in their life, which include a lack of life inside the own family, infection, a brand new glide, or unemployment. A character with a weak spot is an easy target and occasionally the terrific for the psychopath. There are one of a kind psychopaths who need an excessive task. They look for the man or woman that may be a outstanding in form for them. No one is evidence in opposition to the psychopath when they decide to get their hooks into you.

From the outline, you know it's far difficult to decide if someone is a psychopath. You may think that if the specialists can't determine it out after a assembly or with a person, how will you find out in case you are a victim? While it may be hard at the identical time as you're inside the thick of all of it, thru knowing yourself and stepping decrease again to analyze the situations and their developments, you'll be able to decide if some thing isn't always quite proper. If you believe you studied you have determined your soul mate because of the truth the individual mirrors everything you need to pay attention, but leaves you feeling there is a few factor lacking, you then honestly genuinely are in threat of finding your dream shatter right into a hellish nightmare.

Chapter 2: CAB: Cognitive, Affective, and Behavior

Research shows that psychopathy may be divided into 3 businesses: belief, emotion, and movements. These are listed as cognitive, affective, and behavior, respectively. You also can need to think about them as CAB as a way to keep in mind that there are 3 organizations you can use to explain a psychopath's traits. The traits that fit into each elegance are designed on the idea that the psychopath lacks a superego.

Freud turn out to be the primary character to talk approximately psychoanalysis on the idea of the Id, ego, and first rate-ego. The Id is taken into consideration as a "set of uncoordinated instinctual dispositions" someone has. The ego is the organized and practical part of a person, which "mediates some of the goals of the Id and superego. The superego is characterised due to the fact the moralizing characteristic. The superego is consequently the element of the mind's psyche that forestalls the Id from doing the whole lot it wants to do.

The superego is supposed to take the cultural suggestions society has taught them in addition to the ethical steering of dad and mom and their impact to create a block for the Id. It is what Freud known as the "ethical experience" of a person. The superego learns from educators, teachers, and those it considers best function fashions. It is also the part of the thoughts that goals perfection. When the superego is walking appropriately, it contradicts the Id, ensuring that social interactions are within the super manner, in which there may be a feel of right/incorrect, and guilt. The Id is all approximately getting what it needs irrespective of what's morally accurate.

Psychopaths have impulses, desires, desires, goals, an prolonged sexual preference, and aggression, which aren't regulated with the aid of the superego in step with Freud. The loss of the superego is the very motive the cognitive, affective and behavior tendencies searching for to satisfy the psychopath even as usually hurting every other. It is why the psychopath can create victimization plots to harm others for the natural satisfaction of seeing others undergo.

Some of the developments in the ones three commands may be more apparent than others. They are normally discovered out early on, even as others can be hard to study till they're observed out over a long period of time. It is as an lousy lot as you to look for the ones dispositions, have a look at them correctly, and notice the reality of the scenario. Many of the traits healthful on Hare's 20 item tick list, but are explored extra substantial to provide you an concept of a manner to identify them as a regular character and no longer as a psychologist.

Hare's Checklist

? Glibness/superficial attraction

? Grandiose experience of self confidence

? Need for stimulation

? Pathological liar

? Manipulator

? Lack of remorse

? Shallow feelings affected for your gain

? Callous

? Parasitic

? Poor conduct manipulate

? Promiscuous

? Lack of long time dreams

? Impulsive

? Childhood behavior problems

? Irresponsible

? Failure to actually accept responsibility

? Short term relationships

? Criminal versatility

? Juvenile delinquency

? Revocation of conditional launch

As you may see, the gadgets on this list are greater for the psychologist and some you might not be capable of recognize besides the psychopath tells you without delay that they'd adolescence problems, juvenile delinquency, or they have been incarcerated earlier than. Also undergo in thoughts that not all the gadgets in this tick list must be fulfilled for someone to be considered a psychopath.

The DSM V calls for there to be a pattern of "push aside for and violation of any other's rights," character functioning issues together with impairments of self and interpersonal functioning. There need to additionally be at the least a few pathological persona inclinations and dis-inhibition whether all 4 underlying factors have a look at or simplest . In one of a kind words, the individual can be callous and deceitful, but lack open hostility and although be taken into consideration a psychopath. Keep Hare's trends in thoughts in addition to the DSM V requirements as you study the cause of CAB traits in more element.

As you look at thru those tendencies you may want to have Hare's tick list. If you determined you realize a psychopath, live with one, or have met one, you would possibly need to hold this man or woman in mind using the checklist and facts from this ebook to help you find out the way to get out of the abusive scenario you is probably in. Your aim want to be to discover a healthful relationship, where you and your companion are equals—not a scenario in that you're manipulated for the a laugh of the sport.

Chapter 3: In Depth Cognitive Traits

Cognitive traits are defined as "idea" dispositions. Cognitive is defined as "of or referring to cognition; concerned with the act or approach of perceiving, knowing, and so forth." in step with the Dictionary Reference. It moreover says, "of or concerning the mental technique of reminiscence, perception, judgment, and reasoning as contrasted with emotional and violation strategies." What this indicates is the psychopath will lack inclinations that offer proper cognitive processing in terms of judgment, perception, reminiscence and reasoning. Their mind center on getting what they need irrespective of what society considers appropriate.

Lacking in Morals

First up on the list isn't any ethical price. A psychopath is not going to look any charge in following moral or moral measures.

They bear in mind morals to be the unimportant and best for the prey to observe. Their idea method isn't going to have a look at a situation and keep in mind if it's far morally or ethically traditional with the beneficial aid of society. The following question indicates the difference amongst a psychopath and mentally wholesome person.

How could possibly you react if you observed a mom frantically searching out her baby in a branch keep? A mentally healthy individual have to try to help the mom, probably see if she has alerted safety, and if not, try this for her. This man or woman could help because of the truth it's far the morally accurate element to do. A psychopath ought to stand and watch, moreover be amused on the mother's ache. If they knew in which the kid have become they may now not step up to say, till there has been a gain to them.

All are Enemies

The psychopath appears at all of us as an enemy to be used, conquered, and manipulated. Remember those warlords of ancient times? They loved the amusing of conquering their enemy and now and again grew to become at the human beings they had been skilled to defend. Psychopaths are lots like those warlords who've been clearly bloodthirsty. The thrill is in seeing an enemy outwitted and defeated, and everybody is honest game in phrases of who the enemy is.

Perception of Others

Already we realize the psychopath believes honestly all and sundry are enemies, but this additionally coincides with the decision for for perfection from others. If someone isn't perfect, the aggression or abuse can begin. This intolerance of others is going beyond ordinary dissatisfaction. The psychopath will in truth assault the character in preference to the conduct he or she did no longer like. Rather than mentioning the conduct of a few different changed into not warranted, the psychopath is more likely to say "you're horrible, nugatory" or some aspect alongside the ones terms. It is your complete being that is unsatisfactory now not surely the manner you act or the error you made. In reality, his concept goes past making you right right into a horrible person, it's miles going into wondering you are vain to the component of elimination—if the psychopath is aggressive.

The Goal Takes Precedent

The Victimization Plot is usually the primary intention within the mind of a psychopath. He or she feels justified to do what he/she needs, once they want, because of the truth all that subjects is achieving the goal they've got currently installation. The cause may be conquering the subsequent sex partner or as horrible as the subsequent kill.

Grandiosity, Superiority and Entitlement

Along with feeling his aim is the maximum important is the psychopath's assumption that he/she is some distance superior to every body else. A splendid instance of this will be psychopathic leaders like Adolf Hitler. His belief that he had to lead the "correct" race of humans into a ultra-modern generation, whilst additionally being a charismatic leader to influence many into believing it too, indicates how frightening psychopath's ideals in their dreams and superiority can be.

Not simplest does the psychopath receive as authentic with he's superior to others, however this character believes they're first rate, past anybody else. There isn't any boundary to their egotism. Their excessive narcissism can simply assist them cover on the back of various intellectual fitness problems. Narcissism is definitely a fear of grievance and rejection that results in shame, depression, and tension. These aren't emotions or mind a psychopath may also have, however he/she may be capable of have an effect on them. The idea of real narcissism as regards to psychopathic developments is not based totally completely totally on fear or tension in any respect, however a proper notion that he or she is capable of what they declare. There is a very actual choice for the psychopath to believe in their very very personal lie or to take over someone else's identification and the accomplishments of that person.

Superiority and grandiose thoughts are paired with a experience of entitlement. Since the psychopath believes he is a long manner advanced to others and that he has outstanding accomplishments that have to not be sure thru society guidelines, he moreover thinks he is entitled to whatever he desires. He or she's thoughts revolve around this want to have what will excite, please, or at the least try and fill the void they have got.

Thoughts are Never Grey

Most humans have the potential to appearance each different character's aspect to topics. They are able to see the grey in a black and white international. A psychopath cannot see this in any respect. Instead, the psychopath without a doubt sees the black and white concept method. There isn't always any middle floor; it is each or, and if unstable, it could result in excessive damage.

The psychopath never has mind of guilt, responsibility, and they may be very angry if they will be defeated. Winning is a pinnacle priority, or at the least what they understand due to the fact the win. Their essential protective notion is projection with denial and clarification as part of the convoluted sample of wondering. The psychopath is by no means incorrect; it is continuously others who are incorrect and prone.

The mind of a psychopath are by no means delusional. They might probably remember in a lie they have got advised due to the fact they neglect their beyond. The beyond has no this means that that to any psychopath, so if a lie suits, it is some component they preserve to apply. This does not make the psychopath delusional unless the psychopath additionally has a psychotic disorder.

Always preserve in thoughts the precept idea a psychopath has is to damage you, whether or not or not it's far physical, emotional, financial, or non secular. If you are courting a psychopath, that person will harm you, cheat on you, and chuckle at you with the explicit purpose of breaking you down into nothing.

Chapter 4: Affective Traits

Affective or emotional traits of a psychopath can also moreover in some strategies look like the above. Simply endure in mind that the mind a mentally ill individual has also are tied to feelings. The psychopath has a debilitating illness that guarantees they in no manner enjoy emotions. They can have an effect on feelings you need to appearance, however now not keep in mind in them in any respect. When it entails affective inclinations, the psychopath is incapable of attaching to each person or thing. Amazingly, psychopaths can act nicely, displaying feelings you want to look, however they in no way have actual feelings or relationships. One day a switch may be flipped and suddenly the emotions you spot are long lengthy long past. They can lessen you off, stating they never had feelings for you, in no way loved you, and it end up all faux. The first-rate way to look through the emotional lies they challenge is to be aware of their memories. When the psychopath attempts to influence you of his or her love for others and the way it changed into the other character's fault that a dating disintegrated—if you are listening you may see via the psychopath and discover there has been no attachment. Here are a number of the common affective inclinations you need to look for.

Scorn is the Psychopathic Emotion

It has constantly been a wellknown consensus of the psychology network that psychopaths haven't any emotions, but this is not pretty authentic. They do have emotions frequently centering on anger and hate. Scorn is an emotion they surely experience. They have contempt for others and do now not feel others must be taking over location in this earth. Psychopaths additionally experience every person else is not well really worth of approval or apprehend.

Displays Confidence

Confidence is a flowery idea. It may be a belief or maybe a behavior feature. It is likewise approximately the emotions they display. A psychopath will display self warranty for genuinely all and sundry to peer. They are noticeably confident in their ability to manipulate and apprehend human nature. According to George Simon, PhD. And his ebook Untouchable: The Chilling Confidence of Psychopaths "Psychopaths are assured of their potential to govern and understand neurotic humans." It is extra about information everyone; they'll be quite able to knowledge those with intellectual infection, pressure, or susceptible component (because the psychopath perceives it).

A well instance of that could be a serial killer duo. A psychopath can also moreover additionally pick a weaker individual to govern into killing along side her or him. There is continuously a dominating aggressive partner with a weaker, results manipulated helper even as it's far a pairing. The unique individual may additionally furthermore have sociopathic inclinations or any other intellectual infection that offers this character with violent trends. The key component is domination. This domination comes from the self belief the psychopath has in him or herself.

Empathetic Affectations

A psychopath can show empathy. It is an emotion they do now not apprehend and do no longer revel in, but it's miles even though an emotion they could show. The psychopath can region themselves to your thoughts and apprehend precisely how you may react or feel in any given state of affairs. They can display you sympathy even if they do no longer revel in it. Many dad and mom have an emotional empathy for others, but the psychopath has cognitive empathy displayed as an emotional response.

Empathy and the show of it is going back to their potential to lie convincingly. They recognize what we revel in and need, but they only use that to their benefit to lie and deceive as a way of having what they need. So you can't allow your self see their empathy as emotional. Instinctively we want to accept as true with in what others are displaying and saving in phrases of feelings, but realistically it is possible to see the deception. You need to educate yourself to look it. You ought to be inclined to appearance past the act.

Anxiety and Fear Doesn't Exist

Psychopaths do now not revel in fear or tension. They do not worry they may be abandoned thru a few other man or woman due to the truth they will be usually on pinnacle of things. Their self belief and egotism ensures that you are harmed in preference to the psychopath. It poses a large danger to you if they may be violent because of the truth they will not experience worrying or fearful of being caught and punished for their crime. They do not worry what may also additionally seem in the future. A person that has no fear is always a volatile entity to recognize.

Ruthless Emotion

Their feelings are ruthless due to the truth loss way now not anything and they worry now not some component. Love is for fools as is friendship, affection, or sympathy. However, the psychopath can experience frustration in loads of situations. If they may be no longer recognized because the great thoughts they are or a person receives of their way, the psychopath can experience frustration. It can bring about movements like killing a mosquito landing in your arm. You could in all likelihood swat it and ultimately kill it for sucking your blood. When a psychopath is annoyed they'll be capable of do away with the impediment to ensure their purpose may be met.

Final Thoughts on Emotions

An overwhelming fear, have to you meet a psychopath with aggressive tendencies, is their entertainment of no longer having feelings. They view their lack of remorse, empathy, and ruthless actions as electricity. Along with frustration psychopaths can revel in boredom without trouble. When a killer or violent character is bored, they frequently are searching out a manner to give up this monotony. It might also moreover come out as infection, anger, or large rage. If you are worried in a sexual dating, you may experience for a time that this psychopath is in love with you and sees satisfactory you, but you may soon understand it is a supply, and handiest a supply, relationship instead of take. You will regularly see a psychopath display admiration for him or herself due to the fact he's happy with the ache inflicted. These are the feelings that can be displayed.

You will also discover that the emotion of keep in mind is nonexistent in a psychopath. He or she dreams you to just accept as genuine with them, however they will now not do not forget you in bypass decrease returned. Even in case you do now not question them, they may be not going to provide you the emotion that there is full take delivery of as true with. It would possibly likely come out as paranoia, in particular in case you are in a romantic relationship. The character might possibly accuse you of not loving them, of cheating, or of different matters due to the fact they do not receive as proper with you. It isn't fear and often it's far to get you to expose your emotions of whole splendor.

One remaining detail to search for as regards to feelings and psychopaths is animals. Does the psychopath get to recognise your dog or cat? Do you spot him neglecting an animal? You would possibly see him or her walking a dog without care, if it's miles on a leash or runs toward internet page site traffic. In reality, they will stand to appearance what occurs. They find the love we have for animals is ridiculous, however the fact that not each psychopath is that this way. There are a few who can display feelings to cover their distaste and others that in reality leave out their animal if it dies, despite the fact that they had been the best to torment, neglect about or kill it.

Never overlook about approximately that each psychopath is going to display extremely good cognitive, affective and behavioral tendencies. It is the capability to cowl, manage, and show most effective fantastic trends that make it hard to decide out the psychopath, even for specialists.

Chapter 5: Behavioral Traits

Behavior is described as an observable motion, hobby, or reaction that is displayed because of internal or outdoor stimuli. The psychopath has a intention to preserve. Some psychopaths will create a whole lifestyles for themselves sporting their mask of sanity for 3 hundred and sixty five days a 3 hundred and sixty 5 days. Others are not inclined to commit to a regular life. An nameless psychopath as soon as stated any masks one wears will chaff after a while. He changed into concerning wearing an invisible masks to cover his proper self. Some psychopaths are unwilling to position at the masks they invent for too extended. It is a part boredom and issue thrill.

A psychopath who needs some component new is going to ensure to get it thru converting the masks. A psychopath who is content material material in all he or she has based totally on the life and lies created will attempt to preserve it. It is the longer term con of people that starts offevolved to show the real conduct of the psychopath beneath.

It also desires to be stated that the psychopath might not adopt the mask for all people. Sometimes the mask is most effective displayed for the people she or he desires to "win" over in the game. An extra character getting in the way can see the genuine terror of the individual ought to or no longer it is expedient for the cause of the psychopath. Here is an example:

Say you're sitting with a superb pal and her charismatic boyfriend at a restaurant, and he locations your friend down in subtle methods. Since you are not in love, you see this conduct plenty much less tough than your buddy. When she goes to the rest room you observation to the individual that you do now not like how he treats your extremely good pal. The psychopath need to lay on the enchantment, bringing up he simply had a terrible day and at the same time as your buddy comes back express regret. On the opportunity hand, the psychopath should probable find out it a whole lot less complicated to expose their real nature, threaten, or perhaps attack you later so you do not ruin his plan.

While a fictional instance, it's miles one that takes place in real conditions. When it's miles much less tough to hide the real motive, the psychopath will achieve this. Here are some distinctive behaviors that you will be able to spot if you are looking carefully sufficient.

Safety of Anyone is Unimportant

A psychopath does now not have the conduct of protection. He or she can be capable of no longer thoughts in case you are harm or inside the event that they get damage. An instance can be determined in James Fallon. This psychopathic neuroscientist as soon as took his younger son fishing. His different own family emerge as inside the automobile at the time, but they refused to get out due to the "Beware of Lions" signal. The family come to be on excursion in Africa. The more youthful son or perhaps the psychopath have to have met with a lion, however it did now not count number quantity.

It come to be well nicely well worth the fun of the danger. In fact, many psychopaths are danger takers. They need stimulation to fulfill their appetite for pride and fun. Since the psychopath is courageous they do now not mind making unstable movements, whether or not or no longer it is in intercourse, finance, criminal, or journey techniques.

A psychopath may additionally pass skydiving with out instructions. They may additionally additionally climb a unstable mountain pinnacle without right machine. It is plain to many psychologists studying psychopaths that they may sleep around regardless of the results. In truth if they will be identified with HIV, then it is all of the more amusing to have unprotected sex in step with the research. If the psychopath is going bankrupt, takes one million greenback car out and destroys it, or baits a regarded crook, it is eager approximately the amusing, without fear or regard for chance.

Forever Charming

Psychopaths are usually charming and charismatic. Someone searching from the out of doors in might not see this person as captivating, but you'll due to the reality the appeal is layered on in precisely the way so one can enchantment to you so as for the psychopath to advantage their purpose. Often this fascinating behavior is tied to their clean talking capabilities. A psychopath is verbose and fluent inside the language of appeal, but commonly only one skinny layer deep. If you appearance past the captivating demeanor, you could spot this conduct as faux.

Intelligence coupled with Intense Goal Oriented Behavior

The psychopath shows a immoderate level of intelligence, but it is always intensely aim oriented. You may be unaware of the cause, but each element the psychopath does is to carry that purpose to fruition. Once they have a goal in their net sites, the character could have tunnel imaginative and prescient. They might not see a few thing, however the interest is on making you or whomever they goal go through. However, you cannot count on certainly due to the truth they'll be of narrow cognizance that they can't adapt and react to conditions.

If the psychopath is threatened with regard to their intention, they will still make sure it takes area, but they'll regulate the how, together with harming each unique to make certain the motive keeps. The intention is unstoppable in plenty of occasions, whether or now not it's far to obtain custody of kids, getting you right into a courting, robbing a economic organization, killing each different person, or conning you from your money.

Obstacles, specially if you are dealing with an competitive psychopath, must be eliminated. If you end up an smart obstacle to the purpose, it may positioned you in greater damage.

Deceit as a Behavior

Being a pathological liar is a feature. The lies are thoughts the psychopath has and the emotions they show are lies. The behavior is to lie to be able to manipulate and cheat you. The psychopath will do everything it takes to win irrespective of what. Their tremendously aggressive conduct will remain amusing and attractive so long as they are now not threatened or bored.

The Culmination of Behavior

Traits together with being well mannered, argumentative, defiant, smug, expansive, or persuasive are just behaviors that help the psychopath acquire his or her aim. The widespread conduct displayed with the aid of any psychopath is taken into consideration one of control. Whether they need the fashion to be displayed, the clean operator element, or getting a few component through call for, the psychopath will use their arsenal of intelligence, real appearing, and manipulate to ensure what they need is given. Sometimes it takes searching on the large photo to appearance the single tree within the wooded vicinity.

To guard your self from any psychopath in your circle of relatives, pal circle, at paintings, or in a dating you have that permits you to step decrease back, cautiously test the behavior and observe if the wooded region culminates proper right into a assembly of behaviors like the ones listed proper proper right here.

By now you understand that the CAB trends are almost the same, it's miles actually the manner you view them: concept, emotion, or behavior that may make it clearer that there may be a psychopath on your lifestyles. These equal inclinations are the ones highlighted via Dr. Hare and special psychologists, but now you have a more intensive have a look at every of them in an entire lot of specific contextual conditions.

Knowing the tendencies, how they may be examined, and disseminated is honestly the begin. You additionally want to have a study things like relationship flags to help you spot what you might not be seeing quite but. The subsequent financial disaster will observe courting flags that will help you spot a psychopath. Always do not forget that at the same time as behaviors may be displayed as emotion or concept—the psychopath is without worry, judgment of proper and wrong, and inhibitions. He or she will be able to emerge as extremely volatile or may additionally additionally already be a specifically competitive, violent criminal hiding in undeniable sight.

Chapter 6: Relationship Flags

Relationship flags require you to be purpose. When in love that is hard. Most humans want to keep in mind there may be a soul mate to be had for us. Trouble is we no longer frequently discover the person we're seeking out, so at the same time as the appropriate mate comes alongside we need to don't forget within the special man or woman. We get tunnel vision searching at the quality elements of the man or woman, taking issue inside the "honeymoon" section, and whilst the psychopath in the long run indicates his or her real colorings, all which may be left is the damage and betrayal. If you want to keep away from being a victim of a psychopath, then you definately need to check the overall photo. Looking at one trait is not enough. The entire woodland of developments is the only manner to see thru the deception to the actual unemotional character beneath.

Exactly the Prince Charming You Desire

The psychopath goes to fit your idea of a soul mate. They is probably fascinating in precisely the way you need them to be. If you need a warmness, assured, outgoing individual—the psychopath is probably that for you. If you need someone who has a first rate coronary heart but is a touch clumsy, the psychopath can emerge as this for you. When you're the psychopath's aim, he or she will cognizance on you absolutely. The man or woman goes to make certain you are pleased inside the senses and thoughts. They will disable your instincts and obstacles, even help you lose yourself-shielding conduct.

Some who have been sufferers of psychopaths say this diploma is sort of a trance country. You discover your self comfortable, open to idea and wishing to recognition on his or her fascinating behavior. This overly captivating behavior that fits you to a tee is the earliest warning signal.

You are lulled into believing this individual is precisely who you have got been searching out. It is quite risky because of the reality you will forget the opportunity crimson flags. Keep in thoughts that some thing too appropriate to be right often is. A psychopath has the capability to reveal us the good in ourselves and having us agree with they might see it too. They prey in your insecurities and weaknesses with the aid of the usage of being precisely as captivating as they want to be for you.

Relaxed, Always

The psychopath is a loner, however high-quality at being in social conditions. They commonly normally tend to face a thing to take a look at, plot, and plan. However, they commonly make it appear to be they will be part of the institution. The demeanor they show goes to be tension free. In fearful or aggravating conditions they'll no longer display any emotion. This in flip locations you comfy. You may be lulled into a cushty feeling because of the fact the psychopath is making you snug. The intimacy and terms used will make it seem as if you have known the character for years, irrespective of the fact that it has satisfactory been a few minutes.

Discussion Ability for all Situations

The psychopath is continuously excellent at verbal exchange. The excellent topics can emerge as fun recollections. In a courting scenario he's regularly going to do the talking. The psychopath person desires you to be lulled proper right into a sense of protection, and to preserve you in that situation they need to talk.

A psychopath is often going to provide personal records speedy. The memories may be actual or faux, the idea at the lower back of those reminiscences is the intimacy it gives. When someone tells you a few factor right away, it receives you to simply accept as true with them and expose records approximately yourself. It makes you revel in cushty and nearer.

The psychopath is going to show you personal facts to expose that he or she isn't scared of judgment or rejection; therefore, you may moreover be open and inclined with the psychopath. Unfortunately, the psychopath is just beginning you up as a aim so as to damage you.

Happiness is Key

You will begin to loosen up and revel in being glad with the psychopath. He or she can be capable of seem clean going with a laugh reminiscences to inform. The psychopath is hoping you'll see how mundane your lifestyles is and that they are able to make your existence complete of a laugh and happiness. The character targeting you for a romantic relationship dreams you to realise there may be not a few component weighing him down. This individual does now not have a judgment of proper and incorrect, so no longer something gets him down and no luggage of the past can be coming alongside within the courting. It makes you enjoy hopeful and satisfied, because of the fact you understand you aren't with a person who is going to reveal out neurotic, or so that you are lulled into questioning.

Stimulation is a Must

Any psychopath dreams stimulation. This form of person will constantly be busy. If they may be no longer doing some aspect with you, then they're out doing some factor else. To get you into their net they'll want to spend as a first rate deal time as possible with you. When this isn't feasible, they'll discover a new target, possibly having or three at the equal time. If you begin to bore the psychopath, they will move on. You want them to collect this with out harming you, but this is not constantly the case. You actually want to appearance out for a mate this is commonly going and constantly looking you to go together with them along aspect the aforementioned trends.

The Perfect Combination of Affection

Psychopaths provide the affection you are ravenous for. This individual is constantly going to make you enjoy that they'll be looking at you and no character else. They want to be with you in element and might be very bodily in terms in their appeal to you. It might be very viable to expect a number of the best sexual own family contributors may be with a psychopath because of the truth they need you to be lured into thinking you are becoming the whole lot you want. The psychopath dreams the extreme sexual courting to "experience", no matter the truth that they may be in no manner clearly glad.

Their hobby is going to be on you with mobile telephone calls, texts, emails, and in character. You are going to revel in in particular desired. Many who have dealt with psychopaths call this diploma in a courting "love bombing" because of the fact you are totally the middle of their "love." The stage will now not remaining all of the time because of the fact most psychopaths are too lazy to maintain their mask in region for the lengthy haul.

While he can also say he loves you after a date or , it isn't real. It is not the magical Cinderella story which you desire and dream for. Instead he's telling you what you sense you want to pay interest. Anyone who says they love you after only a few dates is presenting you with the maximum important crimson flag of all.

It is exquisite to listen, but you need to no longer have a number one date and gather a mobile cellphone name 10 minutes later with the character telling you they love you. If this takes area run!

It sounds tough as a manner to determine the psychopath from the real character that has emotions. Always consider that a psychopath wants to victimize you and they are trying this thru manipulation. They want to make you fall for them and then turn you inner out for the natural amusing and pride of doing so.

Chapter 7: Secret Manipulation

Psychopaths are the pleasant at covert or mystery manipulation. Many psychopaths are natural at the ones strategies and people who aren't are quite skilled. If you have got ever felt those emotional manipulations, you then definitely have recognized a psychopath.

Reinforcement is by no means Consistent

Most dad and mom are educated on splendid reinforcement. It has an inclination to usually be high-quality reinforcement that we expect at sure intervals, particularly in paintings or whilst there can be an accomplishment that we've got received. For a psychopathic dating, it's miles an awful lot one in every of a type.

Manipulation allows you to advantage effective reinforcement on a random foundation. You may get interest, reward, appreciation, statement of love, and adoration, but it's far in no manner at the same time as you anticipate it. They are also running on doubt, tension and worry. The juxtaposition is to maintain you coming lower decrease returned. You are forced to stay within the courting through the excessive notable reinforcement they provide, and but you're involved that every one of sudden you're going to lose the individual you "love" most. You will find out you are in an up and down emotional situation much like a roller coaster. The manipulation is sincerely sensible due to the reality the psychopath has to exert manage and energy of you. While they scorn love, the psychopath furthermore enjoys seeing you undergo due to it. You aren't some thing greater than a lab rat to the psychopath.

Along with high exceptional reinforcement is going to be terrible reinforcement. You may additionally get keep of the silent treatment, but you have not any concept why. The psychopath could probably live out very overdue every night for a totally long term as a punishment to you. Yet, you have not any concept why the man or woman unexpectedly modified.

As a part of this draw close of manipulation plan, the terrible emotions you experience closer to the individual are returned once more to you. If you bitch or question the person it's far your fault, it's far you who has finished some issue. The concept of the manipulator is to region the focal point back on you and your faults. The psychopath will let you understand there can be a few factor you need to paintings on, possibly your beauty, your feelings, or your tone. You can be placed proper right into a cycle that feels very hard to get out of.

Veiled Abuse

Psychopaths have the capability to make their tone greater stunning, even if they may be being honestly rude. The call-calling is a few issue you recognize and generally may see as a terrible, but the psychopath does it in a manner which you do not see their anger. You sense they may be being sarcastic or kidding, but you still marvel because of the fact the harm and insult is there. However, you are generally lured into believing that the abuse is not clearly abuse in any respect.

Triangulation in a Romantic Situation

One of the remaining things to speak about almost approximately manipulation is triangulation. The manipulator will use distinct human beings in their tactic to damage you. You also can find out the psychopath starts to flirt with a chum or coworker to make you jealous or throw you off balance. The manipulator isn't always going to artwork to show they will be honest. In truth they will want you to enjoy upheaval so they'll placed you in a characteristic to be insecure.

The psychopath does no longer revel in guilt, however they recognize which you do. Guilt and disgrace are two feelings they want you to enjoy because that is additionally going to have power over you. In every of the above conditions that manipulate you, the overall emotions you generally have are guilt or shame. You could in all likelihood revel in shame because of the fact you have been rejected. You could in all likelihood start to get hold of as proper with inside the veiled abuse that would have insinuated you have got been defective. Emotional damage is one of the maximum severe because it chips away at our self guarantee till there isn't always a few aspect left. Worse, the psychopath is an professional at putting off your self perception and top notch emotions approximately your self.

Look at Yourself to See the Puppeteer

It seems extraordinary that you can ought to test your self to discover the puppet strings, or does it? You recognize who you're or who you need to be. You apprehend the man or woman you were earlier than you met the psychopath, which means that in case you study your self and what's happening to you similarly in your emotions, you may often see the psychopathic manipulation. The way you act and experience is a splendid indicator to you as to whether or not or now not or not you're being harmed via the usage of way of a psychopath.

Here are a few highlights that allow you to see the manipulation for what it really is:

? Your love is popping to fear of losing that love.

? You enjoy pressured wherein you used to experience snug and assured approximately your courting.

? You feel happiness is lengthy gone and in its area are desperation, tension and disappointment. Experts name this "manipulative shift."

? You are unhappy, however you can't stand to lose your dating.

? You discover your mood is beginning to rely upon the connection.

? Suddenly a easy courting has turn out to be complex, but you can not find the best motive why.

? You are all of sudden beginning to obsess approximately your courting and are desperate to determine out what is feeling "off."

? You ask your associate if there may be something wrong or at least you have the preference to invite, however enjoy you need to now not. Yet deep down there's some element wrong.

? You are becoming protecting and misunderstood.

? Often you experience angry, annoyed, and at a loss for the unexpected trade in what turn out to be a happy courting.

? Your self perception is beginning to lessen, you sense insecure, and regularly an awful lot less sane.

? Ultimately you begin to revel in responsible and that you lack what your associate expects.

If all or any of those feelings are being felt inside the modern-day relationship you have were given were given or it seems like a circle of relatives/pal relationship you have got were given, then possibilities are the alternative person is a psychopath.

It is difficult to reap a point in which you can see what's occurring to you. There is going to be denial and while you lose self notion, you frequently lose strength to in reality examine the entire of your lifestyles as an observer in place of a player. But if you want freedom, then you definately want to try this—you need to be intention and examine the situation. You additionally need to find out that one friend that started to pick a element your dating or disliked your man from the begin. By locating assist from others you may be ready to discover the freedom you desire from the abusive relationship.

Chapter 8: Sense of Freedom

By now you is probably thinking if your perception of a beyond courting or a present day-day one is inaccurate. You want to determine if the abusive scenario you are in or had been in end up because of a psychopath. There is one way to decide if you have suffered from a psychopath in the past. It is the overwhelming feeling of being "free."

If you end a dating, sigh with comfort, and say to yourself "I'm loose", then you definitely surely had an problem. Certainly it could recommend you have got been in a relationship that did not accept as true with you. There are simply relationships without psychopaths being worried which could result in a experience of freedom. Generally you understand what is incorrect in that courting. It is probably the two of you tried too hard to maintain the extraordinary emotions even as you knew it have grow to be over.

When it involves the psychopath, it isn't about understanding what went wrong or the other character agreeing to the surrender of the relationship. Usually it's far the psychopath who ends it due to the truth they may be bored. If it turn out to be a violent psychopath, you may in all likelihood already understand who the character become due to the reality they genuinely confirmed you. However, if it modified into the greater diffused psychopath that harmed you mentally instead of physically, then you definately definately may additionally additionally still wonder why the individual decided to prevent matters.

If you are despite the fact that in a dating however have doubts, then ask those questions:

Do you sense loose from shame?

Do you revel in free from worry?

Do you experience uncertainty or are you free of it?

Have you started to enjoy inadequate?

Are you unable to specific emotions for worry of the others reaction?

Are you actually being yourself?

A healthy dating is not approximately feeling jailed in an emotional roller coaster. A wholesome dating is one that feels identical without a want to trying to find freedom. This isn't always to say you couldn't want time aside from your companion. If you are a person who likes your location, then you definitely definately may additionally have a feeling of freedom with a ladies' or men' night time day out. When you are in a psychopathic dating, you never simply experience that freedom, even if you are out of the man or woman's control for the short term.

You ultimately recognize which you have changed to in form to the possibility man or woman at the same time as you're in a psychopathic relationship. Instead of being time-commemorated you've got been made to feel unacceptable, susceptible and ripe for the selecting. You started to cover your reactions and emotions for worry that you is probably rejected by means of the usage of manner of the only individual who became purported to love you. You may also even though be feeling this in case you are in a courting with the wrong individual. It goes to enjoy hard to say good-bye to the person, however after a short time you'll begin to comprehend what you've got been actually going thru.

Chapter 9: Concluding Thoughts: Seeking Help for You

Being in an abusive courting, whether or now not it consists of a psychopath or every other shape of abuser, can harm you mentally and physical. Getting out of the relationship unscathed is not some thing a good way to take place. If the connection is already over, you do have scars. If you are beginning to see that it wants to stop, then you'll need to repair what has happened to your shallowness. You will should address your feelings.

You are used to feeling shame because of the psychopath. It is an emotion which can keep you all over again from getting assist, however understand to conquer what has took place and to move on as a higher and extra mature individual you want to stand what has came about inside the past.

There are special techniques you can collect assist. The toughest a part of being in a psychopathic dating is then turning to circle of relatives and buddies, admitting which you were taken benefit of, manipulated and harmed. Those closest to you could already understand what you have got got got long beyond via within the abstract and they'll be willing to help, however your shame and lack of self-self notion can also additionally make it too difficult to get the assist you want from circle of relatives and pals.

You do not want to routinely are searching for the ones closest to you. You are virtually going to experience fear turning to an intruder for help after what has occurred to your psychopathic courting, but simplest you may get the assist you simply want. Only you could decide whilst you are prepared to face what has occurred to you.

When you are organized, there are sources which include many on line forums which can be all approximately victimization thru psychopaths. You can are attempting to find a highbrow fitness professional no longer because of the fact you have got were given an contamination, but because of the fact you want to heal. Post disturbing stress illness or at least a few strain from the connection can impact your healthy way of life. Speaking one on one with a psychologist let you. They assist you to comprehend certain matters about the relationship that this ebook has no longer showed you or beautify what you have got were given decided inside the ones pages.

Eventually you can begin to are trying to find groups in which other patients of abuse permit you to conquer the emotions you have got got. With time you can heal to emerge as the character you've got been or to emerge as someone new, more clever about the "sickos" in the global and defend yourself from an abusive courting in the future.

The American Psychology Association moreover can be of help. The association has many articles, a forum, and individuals. You can look to look if any professional on your location is a member of the APA and take a look at their credentials to make certain you can vicinity your be given as real with in the person that is meant to help you.

Psychopaths have been recounted to idiot even experts. Dr. Hare, Dr. Kiehl and masses of various researchers will let you know that they have sat for the duration of from psychopaths and may no longer have recognised it if they did not have get proper of get admission to to to to the individual time and time over again for his or her research. This technique you have got nothing to revel in ashamed of if you were a sufferer due to the fact no one may be the final "psychopath reader." Psychopaths are too exquisite at manipulation, specially on short-term contact. Only whilst you open yourself as an awful lot as look at the scenario objectively and characteristic long time publicity to the individual can you genuinely see the man or woman for who they're.

WHAT MAKES A PSYCHOPATH?

T

proper right here are a few numerous however regularly used terminologies in psychology that don't normally confuse us until and until someone asks for their concise rationalization. One such expression is 'psychopath.'

Even regardless of the fact that most humans choose out the terms 'mental infection' while describing this psychiatric phrase, it gets pretty tough to mention any more than that. If someone even tries to give an explanation for it any in addition, they often assume as adverse to speak with particular, one hundred% surety.

1.1 - DELINEATING THE TERMINOLOGY OF 'PSYCHOPATHY'

The time period 'psychopath' is used for parents who've a bent to be unemotional, self-targeted, callous, and morally wicked. Moreover, on the same time as this single word isn't always taken into consideration an right analysis, it is despite the fact that time and again revised in clinical settings.

The actual definition of psychopathy is associated with the formal time period 'antisocial character sickness' (ASPD). Originally, psychopaths were defined to be emotionally manipulative, deceitful, and uncaring. However, as soon as thorough studies become completed and ASPD grow to be described to people inside the handiest terms, the actual which means that of the term have emerge as recognized. It was then that humans realized that psychopaths pose a splendid chance to society and not absolutely to themselves. Initially, this discovery led professionals to apply the terms psychopathy and sociopathy interchangeably for some time. However, it grow to be later proved that both terms vary and must be said in completely awesome sports (More on that during segment 1.2).

While the early studies found numerous concrete information on psychopathy, there have been regardless of the truth that a few excessive contradictions concerning a few elements. For example, one-of-a-type studies concluded separate perspectives on how this intellectual sickness office work in human beings.

Many researchers believed that there has been a hyperlink among psychopathy and genetics, this is why it could't be controlled with traditional toddler improvement strategies. In comparison, one of a kind psychiatric professionals believed that psychopaths' behavioral issues stemmed from being subjected to children abuse, parental misconduct, or a few other shape of emotional catch 22 situation. We will talk about this precise state of affairs of battle in extra element within the next few chapters.

Lastly, the preliminary-degree studies made it easy that there may be an complex connection among psychopathy and violence in nearly all times.

1.1.1 - Psychopathy and Violence

Violence is normally described as a 'brutal, bodily pressure.' While this precise description of violence works nicely below maximum activities, we have to extend our minds to different opportunities in terms of psychopathy.

Most people envision a chilly-blooded serial killer in their thoughts after they think about psychopaths. We wouldn't rule this photograph out with the aid of using pronouncing it isn't the fact, because of the truth many psychopaths are, in fact, killers. However, it's simply as essential to identifying that their unfavourable conduct isn't always restricted to this unique factor.

In truth, psychopaths are simply as in all likelihood to emotionally manipulate and damage you as they are susceptible to bodily damage. Most psychopaths don't kill. While they tend to be an extended way greater violent than the overall populace, it doesn't propose each one among a kind psychopath you come upon is probably a assassin.

Moreover, numerous research have evinced that at the identical time as psychopaths may additionally kill, most of them go out of their way to make certain that doesn't arise. We have selected our terms most cautiously to ensure you don't misunderstand this declaration. By pronouncing 'they go out of their way to ensure,' we advocate that it's not because of the reality psychopaths assume that their movements would be categorized as 'wrong' in the event that they pick to murder a person. In fact, they don't want the mess that incorporates this specific act, and that's what compels lots of them to keep away from this sort of behavior.

However, every psychopath wants to have their fill of pride one manner or another. This leads them to pick out emotional violence over bodily violence, which includes playing with exclusive peoples' minds by using manner of charmingly controlling them after which destroying their arrogance from inner.

Simply positioned, psychopaths deceive their goal via making them take delivery of matters which is probably, thru all technique, fake. Once the alternative man or woman starts offevolved trusting them, they show display their real component and emotionally control them until they harm down. While it can sound bland in precept on the identical time as compared to psychopaths' murderous intentions, this shape of psychopathy can leave a lively individual feeling vain from the internal.

1.1.2 - Successful Psychopaths

Besides the senseless violent streak that shadows maximum psychopaths and their actions, we additionally want to be aware of each different aspect of their psychology — their ability to transport in society correctly. We can describe such human beings as successful psychopaths.

Unlike one-of-a-kind psychopaths, those humans are much more likely to get proper into a leadership function in area of behind bars. While they although generally have a tendency to use their extremely good tendencies for the incorrect functions, they choose to manipulate their calamitous social impulses each distinctive manner round. 'Choose' is the operative word right here because it's usually in their control to change facets in a depend of seconds.

Nevertheless, this unusual conduct sample compels us to ask, "If the violence (whether or now not or not emotional or physical) makes psychopaths experience completed and satisfied, why select a outstanding method?"

The reasoning at the back of that is related to a selected function that's part of the Five-Factor Model (FFM), also referred to as the OCEAN version. The FFM shape contains 5 personality tendencies (referred to as the 'Big Five') that take a look at an individual's personality primarily based mostly on clinically-completed highbrow observations.

Below are the five developments within the OCEAN version, at the facet of the developments that every feature represents:

• Openness - A self-analyzing man or woman with an uncommon notion way.

• Conscientiousness - An ethical, accountable, and powerful man or woman with excessive aspirations.

• Extraversion - A socially poised, talkative man or woman.

- Agreeableness - A compassionate, sympathetic, and likable being.

- Neuroticism - An demanding, adversarial, guilt-willing, and irritable man or woman.

Studies show that whilst it is definitely viable for a achievement psychopaths to behave as everyday psychopaths, they acquire relatively higher rankings on 'conscientiousness' based totally on the FFM version. Due to this one trait, they instead select out out to successfully distinguish themselves from the unsuccessful psychopaths. What's more surprising is that maximum of them lead their lives with out getting detected.

1.1.Three - A Psychopath's Coping Mechanism

All in all, it in the long run comes proper proper all the way down to what psychopaths pick out out to be. They can both use their abilities to do nicely for themselves academically and professionally, or they in reality don't need that. Having understood that they're always privy to the steps they take, maximum human beings expect that psychopaths need to even have a coping mechanism for changing or improving their behavior.

However, that's not the case.

Most psychopaths don't feel the want for reforming themselves. Furthermore, they don't agree with there's some element incorrect with them the least bit. Psychopaths recognize that they are designed otherwise from others in large, and that they're exceptional with that revelation. In the quit, if there may be some thing that would reason them to change their opinion or choice approximately a first-rate keep in thoughts, it's after they recognize that their alternatives will effect them in any manner. Moreover, they diploma their self-interest as even though growing a quick-time period or lengthy-term investment, which determines how lots artwork they may be inclined to install to tailor their conduct because of this.

Based at the self-righteous mind they need to justify their behavior, it's typically the humans around psychopaths searching out coping strategies rather than the psychopaths themselves. After all, no individual can cope with a self-centered, unemotional, and callous character with out taking some preventive measures that help them stay within the secure vicinity, emotionally and bodily.

1.1.Four - The Diagnosis

Since we are capable of't label psychopathy as an authentic intellectual sickness or infection, the situation that medical examiners diagnose in such instances is Antisocial Personality Disorder or ASPD. However, diagnosing ASPD comes with its traumatic situations, considering those who want to get medically evaluated don't take delivery of as actual with there's a trouble with them in the first vicinity.

Moreover, maximum ASPD exams can't efficaciously diagnose someone till the age of eighteen because of the fact the worst psychopathic behaviors and dispositions make themselves said in the late teenager years. Nevertheless, highbrow fitness experts observe patients' scientific statistics to start the prognosis even for underage patients. Once medical doctors have assessed a affected individual's statistics, they behavior an in depth intellectual assessment. This assessment is a critical step due to the truth ASPD additionally shows comorbidity with unique intellectual and addictive troubles.

The 'Psychopathy Checklist - Revised' (PCL-R) is one of the generally used exams designed to degree tendencies of psychopathic person disorder in humans. It consists of a twenty-object stock to evaluate whether or now not or no longer a person famous a tremendous behavior, indicating they'll be at risk of placed every body or themselves in life-threatening conditions.

Here are the twenty elements protected in the PCL-R check for decoding someone's socially deviant behavior:

1. Superficial enchantment

2. Grandiose experience of self esteem

three. Proneness to boredom

four. Pathological mendacity

five. Manipulative

6. Lack of guilt or regret

7. Shallow have an effect on

8. Parasitic way of life

9. Lack of empathy

10. Promiscuous sexual behavior

eleven. Several short-term marital relationships

12. Early conduct issues

13. Poor behavioral manipulate

14. Unrealistic extended-time period dreams

15. Irresponsibility

sixteen. Impulsivity

17. Lack of possession for personal actions

18. Criminal versatility

19. Juvenile delinquency

20. Revocation of conditional release

It takes approximately hours for a educated expert to finish the assessment and hand out the rating sheet. Each of the twenty items inside the list is scored on a 3-issue scale: zero being non-existent, one being possibly incidental, and being borderline psychotic.

Usually, most effective psychopaths can get a rating of eighteen or above eighteen. On the contrary, folks that reap twelve and beneath ratings are thoroughly called non-psychopaths. Furthermore, human beings acquiring ratings among thirteen and seventeen may be psychotic however need to be similarly evaluated for confirmation.

1.2 - PSYCHOPATHS - NOT TO BE CONFUSED WITH SOCIOPATHS

Most humans confuse psychopaths with sociopaths at the same time as the versions among their strategies are pretty distinguishing. However, it's furthermore comprehensible to confuse every terminologies until each of these factors aren't studied in element.

As we described in advance in segment 1.1, severa medical examiners used the time period 'sociopath' for a positive period to treat any person posing a chance or a threat to society, bodily and mentally. The reason of the usage of this time period have become to allow society recognise of the functionality risk. The time period 'sociopath' in reality exhibited that such humans had been a risk to themselves in addition to others.

Nevertheless, after project thorough studies, psychologists and professionals concluded that the phrases psychopath and sociopath should not be used interchangeably. As consistent with their reasoning, those terms denote distinct developments and must stay separate. Psychologists had to make aware efforts to make people aware of the particular inclinations to put together them mentally for one-of-a-type situations.

Unfortunately, maximum commoners are but oblivious of the 2 phrases, blending them often because of lack of records.

1.2.1 - The Common Difference Between Sociopaths and Psychopaths

Knowing how to differentiate a psychopath from a sociopath and calling them out on their behaviors is essential for staving off the capacity harm. While they'll be each a danger to society and own almost-similar characteristics, we want to be acquainted with their great natures as properly.

Sociopaths and psychopaths use 'amazing intellectual strategies' to obtain the equal quit. Despite having a similar endpoint, expertise how the minds of such humans perform will can help you extract your self from a possible perilous state of affairs. For the sake of readability, we can use the twenty PCL-R factors in the next segment to illustrate how each terminologies want to be understood and dealt with otherwise.

1.2.2 - Signs of Psychopaths - And How They Differ From the Sociopaths' Approach

1- Superficial Charm

Psychopaths thrive on faking their manner into others' lives for their benefit, the use of their charismatic personalities as an advantage. Moreover, they may be extremely good conversationalists, knowledge precisely which memories to percentage to make themselves appearance pinnacle in exclusive people's books.

On the contrary, maximum sociopaths have trouble wearing a wonderful verbal exchange. Their disability to socialise is due to their delinquent nature and rude mind-set.

2- Grandiose Sense of Self-Worth

Most psychopaths experience entitled to live thru the use of their very very own pointers. They twist others' barriers sincerely because it fits them better. Sociopaths undergo in thoughts themselves above social and moral regulations, inflicting them to have a as an alternative inflated view of themselves that makes them enjoy advanced to others.

Psychopaths realise on every occasion their actions defy the norm, however sociopaths usually tend to now not supply it a concept and act all of a unexpected. Their deeds may additionally furthermore join up to them later, however the damage is finished by means of that point.

three- Proneness to Boredom

Both psychopaths and sociopaths love excitement and dramatization in lifestyles. They find out the chance of getting caught in wrongful, unlawful, and criminal acts interesting. Moreover, they get bored without problem whilst made to duplicate a comparable regular for a long term.

However, as maximum sociopaths behave on a whim in place of planning their acts like psychopaths, they get stuck extra often.

4- Pathological Lying

Psychopaths and sociopaths are at risk of lying. However, at the equal time as psychopaths normally lie to to get out of problem, similarly they generally have a tendency to lie to make themselves appearance top, no matter the fact that it's not crucial. Sociopaths generally usually generally tend to temper the truth only for a selected cause, i.E., to cowl up their crimes. Moreover, they regularly combination their reminiscences and emerge as getting challenged via others due to their constant mendacious statements.

In such conditions, psychopaths can often address their very own and exchange their tale while remodeling the information concurrently. On the opposite, most sociopaths find out themselves stuck of their trap.

5- Manipulative

Psychopaths are best manipulators, as they expertly get people to do what they need from them. They can also even use distinct people's feelings and weaknesses to pressure them exactly wherein they need them to be.

Sociopaths usually discover get into some different individual's head tough due to their loss of interpersonal capabilities. However, they manage to do it in the long run, even without a built-in charismatic person that maximum psychopaths have.

6- Lack of Guilt or Remorse

Psychopaths don't understand the manner to sense ache for others. They even insist that human beings overreact at the same time as their emotions are harm. Consequently, they don't revel in any guilt or remorse for performing the way they do with everyone, regardless of their households.

While sociopaths have an extremely low capability for feeling remorse, the feelings aren't actually missing. They can sense shielding about a limited amount of people in their lifestyles and may even visit more lengths to save you them from getting harm.

7- Shallow Affect

You received't ever see a psychopath displaying real feelings. While they might act at the same time as it serves them well, psychopaths live cold and unbothered maximum instances. For example, a psychopath may display anger or sadness if it lets in them to govern a situation or human beings to their advantage. They will now not give up the ghost until the humans they need to manipulate take shipping of as actual with them. In reality, psychopaths don't revel in such feelings and are performing them to get what they want.

Sociopaths have a low electricity for emotions and displaying emotions, however they are not simply stripped of them. They can revel in anger, unhappiness, and happiness in same measures so long as the character being affected is someone they care approximately.

8- Parasitic Lifestyle

While maximum psychopaths will be inclined to be a fulfillment in life in phrases of being knowledgeable and gainfully hired, a number of them use sob memories to soften their aim for manipulating them. Once they've got their goal underneath their spell, psychopaths take advantage of others' kindness for monetary earnings and not the usage of a regard to how it could have an effect on the other person.

On the opportunity hand, sociopaths are some distance tons a great deal less possibly to have a parasitic way of existence as they lack the temperament to get themselves settled in a social, taking walks surroundings.

nine- Lack of Empathy

Psychopaths are incapable of experiencing empathy, due to this they could't placed themselves in someone else's shoes to narrate with them.

However, a few sociopaths can feel a nice amount of empathy for others, but the hazard of that going on in all fairness minimum.

10- Promiscuous Sexual Behavior

Sex is in no way a loving or emotional act for psychopaths, this is why they will be more likely to cheat on their companions without any remorse. They may also additionally even take part in unprotected intercourse with strangers in spite of being in a monogamous courting.

Despite having some capability to feel first-rate emotions, sociopaths don't located intercourse an lousy lot importance each. It can be very unusual for them to restrict themselves emotionally to one man or woman.

eleven- Several Short-Term Marital Relationships

Psychopaths choose out to get married even as it fits them well. For instance, a psychopath might also also are on the lookout for a financially well-off accomplice completely for securing a lavish life-style or to pay off money owed. However, their real nature receives discovered out to their partners, which regularly results in divorce.

Sociopaths can't usually deceive all people to that quantity. However, while sociopaths are quite sensible and percent some of the psychopaths' intellectual strategies, they have got the same future.

12- Early Behavioral Problems

Almost all psychopaths show off behavioral troubles from an early age. They can also vandalize, abuse, and turn out to be extra violent with their buddies. Moreover, this weird conduct most effective escalates with time.

Sociopaths, no longer like maximum psychopaths, are environmentally inspired, developing their erratic conduct with time. It's most effective within the late teenagers that others generally see the harm they may do while given the chance.

thirteen- Poor Behavioral Control

Psychopaths can't make themselves have a look at policies, even though they're trying to take on a totally specific technique for a reason that blessings them. They struggle to check professional legal guidelines, designing their private along the manner. However, they have got a severely medical thoughts while devising a plan. Hence, even as they'll be got down to harm human beings, no longer whatever can deviate them from their path.

In assessment, sociopaths have unpredictable conduct and a non-existent take care of on planning matters, despite the fact that they'll be aware that their lack of control could likely positioned them in grave hazard.

14- Unrealistic Long-Term Goals

Psychopaths are both deeply driven for succession and make best plans to build up favorable effects or they'll be excessively irresponsible but but strive for unrealistic expectancies.

On the alternative hand, maximum sociopaths aspire to collect lengthy-term dreams but now not regularly make it to the pinnacle because of their erratic behavior and absence of manage.

15- Irresponsibility

Both psychopaths and sociopaths make ensures to make their stand higher in unique humans's lives. However, neither of them feels responsible enough for seeing them via.

16- Impulsivity

Most psychopaths live for fast gratification. That's why they don't commonly assume with regard to what their moves might propose for others, as long as they will be now not being in my opinion affected. They may additionally moreover transfer jobs, purchase a brand new automobile, or even circulate to a ultra-modern town if that's what makes them enjoy better. However, their moves are constantly planned so that they don't damage their lifestyle in any manner.

Sociopaths are the equal, however they don't pre-plan some thing. This lack of preparedness often becomes the purpose in their destruction as nicely.

17- Lack of Ownership for Personal Actions

You might in no way see a psychopath or a sociopath take responsibility for his or her movements. They continuously discover a manner accountable the alternative person for their errors, one manner or each extraordinary.

18- Criminal Versatility

Psychopaths do not forget suggestions as guidelines and prison recommendations as regulations. It's in their nature to devote crimes, be it breaking a riding rule, executing a economic violation, or murdering someone. However, they're trying now not to get stuck on the identical time as task wrongful acts.

While sociopaths recognize why guidelines and legal tips are made within the first place, they don't think about the effects when they violate them. They need on the spot gratification, and they may do a little issue to attain that.

19- Juvenile Delinquency

Psychopaths and sociopaths are a long way much more likely to engage in juvenile crimes in choice to one among a kind greater youthful humans of the identical age organization. In the case of psychopaths, they don't experience for others, and this leads them to dedicate crimes. On the opposite, sociopaths can't manage their impulsive conduct and, ultimately, can't save you themselves from undertaking a misdemeanor.

20- Revocation of Conditional Release

Psychopaths and sociopaths don't hold fast to the constraints of conditional launch after they get released from prison. They both find out processes no longer to get stuck over again, or they keep in rate others for buying arrested in the first vicinity.

1.2.Three - The Psychopath's Strength

After delineating the data that differentiate sociopaths from psychopaths, we are capable of discover the simplest aspect that separates each terminologies. It's the impulsive and erratic conduct in sociopaths that leads them to behave irrationally. However, psychopaths assume more clinically and pre-plan the entirety. This extraordinary feature makes them a greater immoderate threat to society.

In short, at the same time as coping with a psychopath, we have that permits you to mentally apprehend our scenario and be brief to react earlier than it's too beyond due to maintain ourselves from the otherwise catastrophic effects.

THE SHUDDERING HISTORY OF PSYCHOPATHS

'P

sychopath' is regularly used as hyperbole for the phrase 'crazy' in our society. People both communicate approximately serial killers like Jack the Ripper after they communicate approximately psychopaths or gravitate inside the direction of emotionally risky human beings.

However, a part of the hassle is that our know-how of psychopaths is commonly unsuitable. Even after discussing the severa signs and symptoms and signs and symptoms of psychopaths, maximum human beings can't consider how those tendencies may be used for a few component extra detrimental than plotting a homicide. Moreover, we take delivery of as actual with that if an character isn't completely evil at coronary heart, they need to be inherently an terrific man or woman.

However, that's not how a psychopath's thoughts works. It isn't all black and white, wherein some aspect is both right or incorrect of their mind. Everything they do is based totally definitely mostly on an excessive amount of calculated questioning. Moreover, while nearly all psychopaths have similar dispositions, they use them for beautiful one of a kind wishes at the same time as they pleasure in their victories.

2.1 - TYPES OF PSYCHOPATHS TO KNOW ABOUT

In mirrored photograph of the these days mentioned records, we are able to thoroughly end that now not all psychopaths are common 'serial killers.' In fact, we can encounter severa different types of psychopaths in our lives.

Let us walk you thru six of the most common forms of psychopaths to offer a easy understanding of the task rely.

1- The Lover

These psychopaths shower their partners with love and adoration till they begin to receive as actual with them and permit their guard down. Of route, there can be constantly a motive inside the back in their act. In maximum times, psychopaths in the

Lover class ensnare their objectives through multiplied intimacy to get get right of entry to to their coins, homes, or some element that could gain them in phrases of stability.

Moreover, they check their victim's obstacles, eroding them until there's nothing left. As the damage birthday party has already tasted the fairytale with their accomplice, they comprehend they are capable of't label the relationship as a delusion as well. What's even greater jarring is that these psychopaths blame their associate for the destruction in their fairy story lifestyles when they have complete manage over the relationship.

2- The Leader

These psychopaths are what we formally declared due to the fact the 'a success psychopaths' inside the last financial destroy. These people genuinely have a better pressure for perfecting their paintings and mountaineering the agency ladder, both through pitting human beings towards every one-of-a-kind or thru way of doing the difficult art work. However, what is going at the back of closed doors of their existence is a totally unique rely.

In maximum instances, The Leader usually subjects their own family to highbrow and, every so often, physical abuse. Moreover, at the same time as these reminiscences pop out in the open, it's generally the sufferer being categorised as 'crazy' rather than the abuser because of their faux enchantment and outgoing persona.

3- The Paranoid

The Paranoid psychopaths accept as true with that everyone they have interaction with is out to get them. They normally tend accountable the arena for something this is going incorrect in their life. This specific thing can be seen as a extraordinarily wellknown human nature as properly. However, it's the psychopaths' fantasies of making others pay that gadgets them apart and makes them volatile.

four- The Rogue

These sorts of psychopaths are the very best to find out, as they'll be specifically reckless and erratic, and that they push aside special humans's safety without even hiding the truth. They might also abuse alcohol and persuade others that they want saving. In fact, they thrive underneath centered interest and love playing the sufferer no matter being the abuser themselves.

five- The Saint

At a few factor in our lives, all of us find out ourselves face-to-face with camouflaged psychopaths who pose themselves as saints. Many of them paintings inside the 0.33 vicinity to drag off a nice characteristic, which facilitates them escape with their behavior for a long time. Our brains generally conflate clinical medical doctors, health experts, life coaches, and religious figures with being 'giving' people. That's why at the same time as we encounter psychopaths who are the usage of those professions as facades to cover inside the lower back of, we grow to be extra willing to believe them.

As a surrender quit end result, it takes us a large quantity of time to unveil their actual identities. The Saints abuse their recognition to serve their ends and to bend others to their will. Moreover, they fake their competencies until someone detects their odd conduct before they % as an lousy lot as discover their subsequent prey.

6- The Arrogant

The Arrogant psychopaths make their sufferers feel unworthy until they chunk the bait. They are confident in their beliefs and reflect onconsideration on all of us with a one-of-a-kind opinion as imbecile and inferior. Moreover, they act on an impulse to get into their goal's head, sow seeds of uncertainty, and manipulate them using conceitedness and contempt. Once they may be sure they've got messed with the alternative individual's head, they depart them the usage of waves of emotions on their private and set their gaze some location else to look for the following scapegoat.

2.2 - MEET THE TEN MOST-FAMOUS PSYCHOPATHS

Psychopaths are like a misfit organization of people who appear like normal, nicely-natured human beings from the outside.

We often come upon them in some unspecified time in the future of our lives in a single shape or every exclusive. Sometimes, they romance us only to mislead and harm later, as seen within the real crime instances dramatized in Dirty John. Other instances, they will be devils jogging below the facade of a doctor like within the case of Dr. Death Harold Shipman. The unhappy reality is that those laid low with such human beings don't have the physical, emotional, or highbrow power to relay our stories efficiently. We fall below their hoax-appeal and meet the catastrophic stop unknowingly.

We might not be capable of get you the complete shuddering facts of psychopaths in a single financial ruin. However, we hope to deliver our aspect for the duration of concerning how psychopaths walk in our society undetectable, maiming us for lifestyles. So, permit's meet the pinnacle seven famous psychopaths of all natures and temperaments to again up the records related to the special sorts of psychopaths.

1- John Wayne Gacy - 'The Party Thrower and Clown-Dresser'

To his suburban Chicago friends, John Wayne Gacy have end up the first-rate subsequent-door guy who cherished throwing block events and completed as a clown at kids's activities. However, they didn't understand that their glad-pass-fortunate neighbor come to be secretly hiding in simple sight.

In 1978, police received a warrant for looking John Wayne's residence due to the fact he changed into the ultimate one to be seen with a fifteen-one year-vintage lacking boy. It modified proper right into a identified reality that the teen was hoping to enroll in his production business for work in some unspecified time within the future. During the raid, police determined numerous articles of apparel belonging to awesome extra youthful men who had additionally been mentioned lacking. Moreover, after they tracked the putrid scent to a four-foot flow slowly vicinity under his residence, they have been revolted to discover twenty-9 decomposing our our our bodies of teenager boys who have been brutally raped and murdered.

Upon thinking Gacy's ex-wife, investigators located out that she often complained approximately the repulsive scent to her ex-husband for years. However, he constantly advocated her it emerge as because of mould growing inside the basement. In addition to the our our bodies observed at his house, John similarly admitted to killing numerous men, whose our bodies he disposed of in a close-by lake.

When his case went on trial, he tried to provide an madness safety, which modified into right away rejected. He have turn out to be convicted on charges of committing a entire of thirty-3 murders and achieved thru using deadly injection in 1994.

This case suggests us how psychopaths motive destruction of the worst type with the aid of manner of providing themselves as the high-quality shape of charmers.

2- John Meehan - 'Dirty John'

John Meehan modified right into a nurse anesthetist and conman, who we are able to with out issue categorize as 'The Lover' psychopath. He have become acknowledged for successfully pulling off coverage scams and bogus court docket instances. However, what got him the maximum interest grow to be his multiple relationships with women.

John Meehan spent a widespread a part of his existence fooling ladies and making them fall for his fake attraction. On his first date with Debra Newell, 59, who ran an up-and-coming indoors format enterprise, Dirty John knew better than to permit go of this life-setting opportunity. After all, Debra exuded wealth in her immoderate black Gucci heels, Chanel bag, and style style fashion designer denims. John right now preferred to get below her umbrella to advantage the blessings.

At first, Debra perception that John Meehan changed into a chunk eccentric, sporting his surgical gloves everywhere he went. However, she shrugged it off, thinking he grow to be perhaps a touch too committed to his process. Moreover, as fast as she changed into in complete awe of John and creating a tune praises of his first-rate and loving man or woman, they have been given married in 2014, a mere one month after their first assembly!.

Later, in 2015, Debra determined that the entirety he had advocated her, along side being an finished health practitioner and saving many lives in the Iraq warfare were blatant lies. In truth, he changed right into a convicted criminal with drug-related costs and coverage scams in his mile-extended listing of crimes.

Their relationship took a downhill after that, and Debra ended the marriage, filing for a restraining order in competition to her ex-husband. However, the order have been given denied at the same time as the decide stated that there has been no drawing close danger to difficulty it.

However, in June 2016, Dirty John stole his ex-spouse's automobile to burn it, irrespective of the fact that he failed. Two months later, he attacked Debra's daughter, Terra, in a vehicle parking with a knife. To his surprise, Terra fought decrease again to shield herself, managed to capture the knife out of his hand, and stabbed him to lack of life. That emerge as the save you of Dirty John.

John Meehan's story have become a warning for women to be careful of psychopathic, plotting to take advantage of them. This actual-life incident became later chronicled and publicized in a podcast, which have become later tailor-made proper right into a tv collection.

3- Harold Shipman - 'Dr. Death'

Now, allow's talk approximately one of the maximum common styles of psychopaths in our society - The Saints. One of records's soul-quavering serial killers concealed underneath the masks of a nicely-reputed British doctor Dr. Harold Shipman. His murderous spree commenced in 1972 whilst he managed to break out with killing at least seventy-absolutely one in all his sufferers at the same time as running at his first workout. Double this quantity, and also you'll get the massive form of sufferers he killed at the equal time as working at his 2d exercise that he joined after butting heads together together with his previous colleagues who positioned him instead brusque, conceited, and conceited.

In 1988, 26 years after his first kill, every a nearby undertaker and each different medical doctor found the extraordinarily high amount of cremation certificates that Harold Shipman had signed off on. Moreover, they noticed strikingly comparable reasons of death for his extremely-modern patients. This emerge as enough to open an research closer to him. However, the initial research modified into poorly dealt with, permitting him to kill 3 extra times.

Nevertheless, Shipman ran out of true fortune later that 12 months even as his closing victim's daughter accused him of not first-rate killing her mom however furthermore developing a faux will under her call, naming him as her sole beneficiary. The victim end up now not buried at that time, bearing in thoughts an autopsy to be ordered right away. This autopsy discovered immoderate levels of diamorphine in her gadget. It became later determined that maximum of Dr. Death's sufferers were killed the usage of the same approach.

Formally charged with fifteen murders but leaving a facts of about hundred and eighteen patients in his wake, he changed into sentenced to lifestyles with out parole in 2000. In 2004, Shipman become located useless in his mobile; he had devoted suicide. However, he in no manner admitted to his other killings at some point of the time he lived.

4- Ted Bundy - 'The First-Ever Televised Murderer On Trial'

Anyone even remotely familiar with the idea of psychopaths is familiar with the call Ted Bundy.

Attractive, well-knowledgeable, high-quality, and brimming with appeal - each of his abilities made him even more no longer going to be a chilly-hearted serial killer than the remaining. His right now likable persona made accepting his a long time-prolonged killing spree more difficult to consider.

Ted Bundy had a hard children; he didn't understand his father's identification and have become raised believing that his grandmother became his real mom. In fact, his real mother was his sister. He went without delay to graduate from the University of Washington with astonishingly excessive grades.

Soon after, he started to behave upon his psychopathic impulses and started out out what ought to most effective be defined as 'the multi-united states homicide spree' in 1966. Bundy's number one suspects have been appealing college students within the Pacific Northwest. He later persisted to gravitate toward Utah and Colombo to aim severa women earlier than he in the long run were given arrested. However, regardless of being charged with a excessive kidnapping crime, he controlled to break out police custody times. He then moved to Florida in which he killed many contributors of a sorority. His very last victim end up a twelve-12 months-vintage female who he raped and murdered.

Ted Bundy modified into in the end captured at the same time as he changed into on the run after killing his ultimate victim in a stolen automobile. However, his trial quick have grow to be a media sensation, and he received a big following. Ever the charmer, Ted continuously welcomed reporters in his cellular to interview him on the equal time as receiving numerous letters of appreciation from his admirers. He later married the sort of admirers!

Moreover, he gave out a long listing of guidelines to find distinctive murders he should probable have committed, a ploy to put off his execution. However, it didn't art work in his decide on in the end. He became finished on the electrical chair in 1989, and his right quantity of patients remains unknown so far.

5- H.H. Holmes - 'The Owner of Murder Castle'

Don't confuse this particular Holmes with the well-known detective, because of the truth you'll most likely be sorely disenchanted. H.H. Holmes spent the instances in his early career as an insurance scammer and later moved to Illinois to art work as a pharmacist. It became there that he secretly have become his 3-tale resort proper right into a homicide fortress.

The place grow to be organized with gas traces, hidden peepholes, lure doors, vain-surrender hallways, soundproof paddings, and thriller passages. Moreover, he even had a surgical desk, a medieval rack, and a furnace to torture and get rid of his patients later on. Young ladies were his favored preference for bringing once more to his lair to have his way with them, however his choice of sufferers come to be now not restrained to them. After luring the unlucky individuals to the homicide castle, he asphyxiated them with poisoned gasoline and then took them to the basement to perform ghastly experiments. Once finished, he disposed of the our bodies in his furnace or skinned them to sell the skeletons to clinical schools.

Furthermore, Holmes have come to be involved in severa coverage scams, accumulating cash illegally from lifestyles insurance businesses. However, he have become stuck at very last for the duration of one in every of his frauds whilst he did not deliver the pay-out. He have become formally convicted for murdering four humans but confessed to twenty-seven extra killings in advance than he became finished through the use of putting in 1896.

Holmes' captivating dispositions and realistic character led him to break out with crimes for numerous years earlier than he in the end got stuck. Nevertheless, he is a primary example of methods psychopaths live amongst us, and we best studies in their proper nature once they make a tiny slip-up and get caught. However, taking the harm they do into interest, we want to train ourselves to stay safe.

6- Ian Robert Maxwell - 'Suspected Spy and Fraudster'

Ian Robert Maxwell is the ideal example of a person carefully coping with themselves as a public decide at the identical time as concealing darkish secrets and strategies and strategies with a black coronary heart. Learning approximately his modus operandi might permit you to recognize how psychopaths conceal in simple sight, and no one even tries to keep in mind them as any much less than normal.

Born in Czechoslovakia in 1923, it didn't take a bargain for Robert to make a call for himself, being a British media owner and an lively Member of Parliament for Buckingham amongst 1964 and 1970. He done those roles for society's sake to return off as a respected citizen even as he turned into a suspected secret agent and a specific fraudster.

He died in 1991 beneath mysterious activities, and his lack of lifestyles stays a thriller to in recent times. While it is believed that he dedicated suicide, there are several unanswered questions as to how he took his life. Moreover, after his loss of lifestyles, it changed into found out that he had siphoned masses of hundreds of dollars from his agency's pension finances. The super element about this specific case is that most newshounds remained remarkably silent about the accusations fired his way in place of doing a little factor about it. Even some of the companies that benefited from Robert Maxwell's movements grew to emerge as a blind eye closer to any hard proof that might have correctly grew to become his 'suspected' call into 'tested.'

We can name Ian Robert Maxwell a successful psychopath whose borderline psychotic conduct compelled him to progress in his field and remained undetected till after his dying.

7- Tom Skeyhill - 'The Blind Soldier-Poet'

A cloud of suspicion has been hovering over this call for a long term now. Looking into the matter from the outside, all you can see is an acclaimed Australian conflict hero, famously referred to as 'the blind soldier-poet.'

During World War I, Skeyhill operated as a flag signaler, this is taken into consideration one of the battlefield's riskiest positions. However, after being blinded because of a bombshell detonation encounter, he lost his sight and changed into transferred out. After that, he composed a poetry-primarily based absolutely ebook about his struggle revel in and toured Australia and america to recite his poetry and fascinate the goal marketplace. Moreover, not extended after the warfare modified into completed, his blindness disappeared following a scientific approach in America.

While the story is heart-touching, numerous reporters and medical subject specialists raised their doubts time and again concerning the soldier's blindness. According to the biographer Jeff Brownrigg, Tom Skeyhill modified into a 'draw close of deception' who faked blindness to avoid fight.

That's now not all. Skeyhill even spun a few massive self-aggrandizing lies to sell his call. For instance, he spoke about his ugly warfare enjoy at Gallipoli whilst he had first-class been there for no extra than eight days and mentioned assembly deceased excessive-profile military people without any evidence to show for it. Although Skeyhill never received a intellectual evaluation, most researchers accept as true with that psychologists may want to have had little to no hassle spotting him as a traditional case of a a fulfillment psychopath.

2.Three - OUR FINAL THOUGHTS

From a lover to a soldier, from a clinical doctor to a random glad-move-lucky neighbor, we meet specific psychopaths but may additionally want to in no manner distinguish them aside. Why? Because irrespective of the image we create in our minds regarding psychopaths, they're similar to us from the outside. The worst element is, masses of them take us from our normal lives and into the lair of destruction without being detected, and no longer long after, they are seen centered on their subsequent victim.

The purpose of sharing the ones real-lifestyles memories of famous psychopaths is to offer our studies-based content material cloth an placing ahead nod, depicting how we've been residing in an undesirably unpredictable society. It's high time to spread attention regarding this crucial rely and encourage mental education for all, much like how we've been promoting self-protection learning to defend ourselves bodily from dangers within the out of doors global.

HOW THEY SEE THE WORLD

P

sychopathy is generally characterised in phrases of diagnostic tendencies. High intelligence, horrible judgment, superficial appeal, the incapacity of love, compulsive mendacity, pathological egocentricity, manipulative conduct, loss of guilt or regret, low willpower, criminal versatility, and grandiose experience of self esteem are some of the pinnacle dispositions of psychopaths amongst numerous others.

AS A CONSEQUENCE of the set up standards we've created for psychopaths, we regularly find out ourselves imagining a chilly, heartless, and inhuman man or woman even as painting a stylish photograph. In our minds, they will be with out feeling any regular feelings like unhappiness and empathy. However, to decide whether or now not our assumptions preserve any water or now not, we must see if all psychopaths percentage the same number one nature from starting or are they remarkable hardwired that manner because of a annoying beyond.

UNLESS WE DON'T WORK on locating the sore spot from in which psychopaths input our society, we can't desire to differentiate the reason for their life successfully. Hence, in this financial smash, we'll talk the following enigmas:

IS it viable for psychopaths to be self-conscious in addition to regretful for his or her callous tendencies?

Is there a hyperlink amongst psychopaths suffering secretly and their final destructive actions?

Does genetics have had been given a few issue to do with psychopaths' conduct?

Can the normal psychopathic conduct be justified with the aid of manner of using professional scientific opinions?

3.1 - SELF-AWARENESS AND REGRET

"Do psychopaths understand that they'll be psychopaths?"

THIS IS one of the most common yet interesting questions humans ask after they first discover about psychopathy. Considering that a psychopath's trends are often known as poisonous, toxic, and unfavourable, most people anticipate there should be no self-consciousness factor in such humans.

MOREOVER, based at the records we've furnished thus far, you could have obtained combined messages regarding this inevitable query's solution. However, this blended reaction come to be unavoidable up until now, as there isn't a right away "certain" or "no" solution to this question. Furthermore, earlier than responding to this complicated seize 22 state of affairs, we needed to begin at the very basics of psychopathy, expertise we are able to't jumpstart in this concern rely variety with out putting in place a valid base.

HOWEVER, now that we've greater than enough records concerning how psychopaths characteristic, allow's apprehend how they see the area from their perspectives.

three.1.1 - ARE They All the Same?

AT A BASIC LEVEL, we can say past an low-value doubt that each one psychopaths recognize in some unspecified time in the destiny that they anticipate and behave in a special manner from others. Figure such variations out might also moreover take them a while, however they in the end see how they could't sense or precise emotions like others. During this time, the psychopath goes thru numerous mental ranges, like confusion and contemplation, to in the long run gather reputation.

THE CONFUSION ARISES after they recognize anyone except them is reacting in any other case to precise occurrences.

At first, they ignore it. However, encountering such conditions again and again, they begin to ponder and offer some critical notion to the whys and hows of it.

Unsurprisingly, their first reaction is suspicion. Mostly, a psychopath's befuddled concept manner progresses within the following way for knowledge others' reactions: They (people) need to be overreacting unnecessarily. Otherwise, why don't I enjoy a few element out of the regular whilst others do?

HOWEVER, when they see the most rational of humans reacting otherwise than how they may in a given situation, simplest then comes the terminal popularity. It's then they understand that they will be set apart from others, and this expertise opens them to discover an entire new international in their very very own.

CONCLUSIVELY, at the identical time as some psychopaths are most effective alternatively aware of the variations among themselves and the rest of humanity, others have a more unique statistics in their state of affairs. However, in every times, the trouble of regret is totally or at least in component non-existent.

three.1.2 - THE CHOICE

IT CAN FEEL like being stuck between a rock and a difficult vicinity for psychopaths whilst they may be capable of't differentiate one trouble from the alternative that maximum human beings outline as feelings, empathy, moral experience, and remorse. In this 2nd, the predatory nature of psychopaths evolves, as they come to recognize that their notable capabilities can art work of their decide upon quite nicely.

MOREOVER, it's furthermore the factor of no return wherein they ought to make a aware choice concerning how they may choose to apply their talents. It offers some of them a clean path to turning into a success within the paintings zone, knowing they'll be capable of do morally unscrupulous subjects without a 2d idea. On the alternative, others pick out to take a unique approach and use their dispositions in techniques that could simplest be referred to as exploitatively unpleasant.

IT'S ULTIMATELY their preference how and for what reason they make use of their high-quality tendencies. In any case, they cover their great nature incredibly, thinking about that maximum people mistake their thrill-seeking out conduct and impulsivity for enthusiasm and the capability to multitask with a committed popularity.

3.1.Three - Real vs. Fake

ONE OF THE maximum complex topics in existence is distinguishing a clever, skillful psychopath from a median, ardour-pushed character. Nevertheless, some signs and symptoms and symptoms help us spot a psychopath. Spotting one could in all likelihood require us to pay hobby and no longer brush aside the accrued statistics, sweeping them underneath the elegance of personal paranoia. We will talk those symptoms in the subsequent financial catastrophe.

THE CHOICES that psychopaths make of their life are in particular based upon what they advantage from their actions. More often than now not, all their moves, even folks that help others, are based on faux values. However, we wouldn't skip as a protracted manner as saying that all psychopaths are the identical on this element.

THAT'S BECAUSE, in some times, a few factors come into play on the identical time as a psychopath has the selection to choose amongst or extra alternatives. Among the pinnacle of these attributes is their upbringing. However, this uncommon discovery leads us into a whole other difficulty count, one which we can cowl in sections three.2 and three.Three. That's in which we're in a position to speak psychopaths' normal beyond sufferings and the way their upbringing topics in the end.

3.1.Four - FROM PSYCHOPATHS to Hardcore Social Predators

WHILE IT'S unusual for psychopaths to be known as upon for his or her demented behavior, they're no pushover confessors. As quick as someone begins carrying down their not unusual feel or ideals, they flow into the yardsticks and improve their act in place of enhancing their cunning persona.

Bending the fact comes to them on impulse, and that's exactly what separates them from sociopaths.

YOU SHOULD KNOW that now not all psychopaths grow to be serial killers or hardcore predators. However, from time to time their contemptuous detachment and tendency to make their sufferers collapse on the seams cause them to train themselves approximately ordinary human conduct after which using this know-how in their schemes and guileful acts. Moreover, the extra we confront them without delay, the more they placed up a foolproof and convincing facade, all of the even as locating new strategies of duping their opponent with vengeful plans.

THAT'S ALSO why we don't advocate tough a psychopath without a constructive path of motion. Since they've got a parasitic person, it provokes them into appearing out even extra once they locate a person's entire hobby targeted on them.

3.2 - PAST SUFFERINGS

We now comprehend how a psychopath's thoughts operates to a positive diploma, and we can keep to speak approximately the priority rely in extra detail as we make improvement in the route of the e-book. However, it's miles despite the fact that uncertain whether or no longer or no longer the mind and impulses motivating a psychopath's movements have had been given some thing to do with their upbringing or past sufferings.

AS PER STUDIES on this count, many psychopaths, like healthy people usually generally tend to like or at least take care of their family and buddies of their early years. However, they've a hard time trusting the rest of the world, it really is a outcome of some hidden struggling.

Gradually with time, their behavior turns more deviant, and they lose all feelings and morality.

FURTHERMORE, there was widespread studies concerning how psychopaths typically have had mainly disturbing or even disturbing pasts. The preliminary motives barring them of their emotions can also consist of the loss of life of a cherished one, abusive dad and mom or stepparents, mother and father' divorce, or some exclusive unbearable element. However, even as such activities are a place to start, that's truly not the end in their distressing times.

THE CONSTANT UPSETS of their lives, in particular an unstable upbringing or ancient beyond, are tremendous catalysts, playing the most unfavorable role in the giant set of sports.

3.2.1 - Emotional Pain

LIKE MOST PEOPLE, psychopaths have a deep yearning to be loved and cared for in their young human beings. However, at the equal time as their desires stay unfulfilled, they take a darkish flip very quickly. It gets even more hard for them to hook up with any man or woman because of the fact their intrinsic man or woman tendencies don't normally in shape the ones of others. Over time, they grow to be aware about their lack of capacity to speak with others and the effects they have got on others, This popularity leads them without the potential to shape strong emotional networks.

THAT'S ALSO why common threads in most psychopaths' histories consist of chaotic family lives, terrible relationships, lack of parental interest and steerage, and unfavorable delinquent conduct that they later camouflage inside the again in their deceivingly faux identification.

three.2.2 - Violence

SOCIAL ISOLATION and absence of ethical steerage regularly precede violence. There comes a factor in a psychopath's existence whilst their beyond sufferings motive them to accept as true with that the entire world is in the direction of them. As they age, they come what may additionally moreover end that they deserve particular treatment and privileges to fulfill their dreams. They justify this line of concept by using the use of citing that it's their right to live freely after being disadvantaged because of their unfavourable instances.

SUBSEQUENTLY, their criminal acts end up greater weird with time as their loneliness turns into notably painful for them. For example, permit's take Jeffrey Dahmer, a convicted American serial killer, cannibal, and sex wrongdoer. In one interview, Dahmer said that he without a doubt killed to have a few enterprise. He didn't much like the act of killing itself, however he knew the vain wouldn't depart him, in contrast to the dwelling. In reality, he tried to sedate his patients first, injecting acids into their brains inside the desire of turning them into zombies. When that didn't artwork, he killed them, talked to them for hours in advance than ingesting their our bodies. According to him, it changed into his way for his patients to stay in addition inner his body.

FOR THE REST OF US, we are able to't endure in mind experiencing loneliness so painful that it drives us to kill. However, psychopaths create their very personal sadistic universe to avenge their moments of abuse, rejection, forget about about, humiliation, and emotional struggling.

3.2.3 - SELF-DESTRUCTION

Violent psychopaths pose a excessive risk to others in addition to themselves. From beyond incidents, we're able to see that such people feel as though all lives are nugatory, which incorporates their personal. Moreover, research has tested that a large form of psychopaths live a as an opportunity quick time as soon as you have got psychologically evaluated. Most deaths in such conditions are associated with risky driving, drug abuse, and involvement in unnecessarily dangerous conditions.

3.Three - GENETICS AND PSYCHOPATHY

We have mentioned that psychopaths' upbringing and their beyond sufferings play a critical role in developing their character traits, there can be one query that still stays a catch 22 situation. Is it possible to have an underlying herbal purpose for psychopathy?

Psychopathy is one of the maximum researched and nicely-studied persona issues. Gradually, with time, statistics and enigmas associated with this subject are being clarified via experimental and psychological opinions. The connection amongst psychopathy and genetics is this sort of quandaries that we have remained harassed about for a long term. However, within the moderate of new studies, we're in a position to finish their correlation beyond a shadow of a doubt.

Research has advised that the mind segments that actively approach feelings, along with the amygdala, insula, and ventromedial prefrontal cortex, display reduced hobby in human beings with psychopathic developments. This impaired capability affects our mind's capacity to shape institutions a number of the stimuli and effects. Does this thoughts impairment turns a person right into a psychopath, or is it their conduct that in the end adjustments their brain?

After project severa thorough neurological investigations, it became understood that the question of nature vs. Nurture in psychopathy isn't that easy to answer. While an person's distressing upbringing and beyond trauma are of the most important elements that in addition enhance their probabilities of becoming a psychopath, genetics also can input this communique in masses of instances.

In fact, youngsters brought up in a nice surroundings can also have the tendency to test their waters, experimenting with others' moral limits is often considered inhumane, in particular at their age. Case in difficulty: we are capable of't continuously blame a psychopath's past for their socially and ethically unacceptable actions. Sometimes, it's in their innate nature to play with other people's minds to stay entertained.

Whether a person becomes a psychopath due to genetics, past trauma, or a mixture of both, they continuously have it in them to control their repulsive impulses. This essential element must not be left out.

Moreover, psychopaths realize all too nicely a manner to apply emotional sufferings in both case at the equal time as often the usage of it to their gain for manipulating others. They understand folks that enjoy empathy will do a little aspect for them as long as they realise the manner to play their playing playing cards just proper. The worst problem about this state of affairs is that it's difficult for others to cut them out in their lives after understanding that they've had a hard beyond, as it makes them experience sorry for the psychopaths.

3.4 - THE NEUROSCIENTIST WITH AN ASTONISHING SELF-DISCOVERY

To placed our research into further context, allow's study the case of famous neuroscientist James Fallon who made an lovely self-discovery one afternoon in October 2005. At the time, Fallon changed into task a study related to serial killers, discovering how their minds operated. While he emerge as sifting thru a chain of PET scans to find out anatomical styles correlated with superb psychopathic dispositions, he determined out how psychopaths' brains showed decreased activity in their backside frontal lobe, this is related to morality and empathy.

Out of serendipity, Fallon modified into moreover acting Alzheimer-primarily based completely research at the identical time. He had each other pile of thoughts scans scattered on his desk that he had accumulated from anyone in his own family for this reason. When he went via that particular stack, he couldn't receive as authentic with what he located. On one of the sheets modified right into a brain experiment that showed obvious signs and signs and symptoms of psychopathy.

Knowing that the check belonged to taken into consideration virtually one in every of his circle of relatives members, he rechecked an appropriate PET tool to discover for an errors. However, to his surprise, it became jogging perfectly. Considering that the take a look at become, in fact, correct, he proper away seemed up the take a look at code to look who it belonged to. Consequently, he end up met with an unsettling revelation - the PET check he have become looking at turned into his very personal.

While lots of us could have hidden this discovery, James Fallon had no trouble the least bit pronouncing this startling fact, labeling himself a psychopath. It is probably due to his boldness and disinhibition, each of which might be commonly associated with psychopathy that led him to talk bravely approximately his finding in an open TED Talk. That considerably-identified consultation have grow to be soon observed with the useful resource of a e-book that he published approximately his enjoy, The Psychopath Inside. In his ebook, he reconciles how someone like him - a luckily married, own family guy - also can proportion and show similar anatomical patterns as a killer psychopath.

He in addition elaborated that he had by no means killed or raped all and sundry in his life nor did he have any desire for those topics. That's why his first concept after this discovery have grow to be to discover whether or not or not his hypothesis come to be incorrect, which might suggest that human mind sports have been not reflective of psychopathy.

However, even as he did a chain of genetic tests, he want to look that he had all the excessive-risk alleles for violence, aggression, and espresso empathy. Based on the neurological and conduct studies he finished upon himself, he knew, as a truth, that he changed into in reality a psychopath.

After a while, he advised the media that it shouldn't have come as a surprise to him to be a psychopath, as he stated that the power of manipulating others had always attracted him. Also, his family facts end up connected to seven alleged murderers.

In considered taken into consideration one in every of his verbal statements, he stated, "I'm obnoxiously competitive. I don't permit my grandchildren win video video games. To be sincere, I'm form of an asshole, and I do jerky topics that piss people off. But even as I'm competitive, my aggression is sublimated. Because I'd alternatively beat someone in an problem than beat them up."

So, the question that puzzled him was - When he should temper his behavior, why did others with similar intellectual dispositions become in jail?

It became after some time that Fallon discovered out the purpose within the again of it. He believed that his adolescence and the manner he modified into added up avoided him from heading inside the route of a scarier path. He stated he became cherished and protected for so long as he should undergo in thoughts. Because his parents were via a sequence of miscarriages, they gave him even extra interest and affection than regular kids normally did.

Fallon's upbringing stored him from stepping into a journey of destruction no matter the fact that he turned into genetically programmed to have psychopathic dispositions. Moreover, there was a third element further to genetics and environment that performed a crucial function in his choice-making abilities - free will.

Case in trouble, Fallon writes in his e-book that when locating this issue of his life, he had been making efforts to try to change his behavior. He consciously stepped as much as do topics which is probably regarded as moral at the same time as taking special human beings's feelings under interest.

However, he does not name himself a saint thru any way. Later, after his discovery, he explained, "I'm no longer doing this due to the fact I'm suddenly notable. I'm doing it due to pride - because of the reality I need to reveal to everyone and myself that I can pull it off."

This is one of the maximum relatable real-existence examples that sums up the whole thing we've mentioned on this e-book up until now, which includes psychopath's violent inclinations, their upbringing, beyond sufferings, genetics, and ultimately, their preference.

Furthermore, to reply whether or no longer or no longer a psychopath's erratic behavior is justifiable or no longer, it want to be self-obtrusive with this situation study. Considering that all psychopaths have manage concerning their moves, they need to be held chargeable for their crimes. After all, they choose out to take the wrong path at the equal time as knowing the results. After all, most a success psychopaths use the equal traits as serial killers, but they don't end up hurting others on this manner, mentally or physical.

DO YOU KNOW A PSYCHOPATH?

W

e have already set up that most psychopaths understand even as they may be special from others, even though it takes them a while to come returned decrease back to that give up. Moreover, the extra intellectual ones who apprehend what the term 'psychopath' consists of even test books to train themselves on the difficulty genuinely to gain an element.

They use that statistics to tackle board what makes them outstanding from others. It enables them cover themselves better in society on the equal time as they preserve to control others to their coronary heart's content material cloth fabric. Furthermore, they will by no means enjoy the want to alternate their behavior if that's what fits them better. The best contradictory case is while psychopaths have a similar thoughts-set that James Fallon dominated via, i.E., searching to reveal to others that they may 'pull it off' with out affecting others. However, except the ones fairly uncommon times, psychopaths see no reason for growth or change.

In truth, maximum psychopaths use every little little little bit of facts they're capable of collect to appearance down on everyday humans, categorizing other's emotional dispositions as restraints. They hyperlink having a experience of right and incorrect with being mentally vulnerable, all of the at the identical time as looking at others' feelings to build up records that could help them play their cards greater efficiently.

Based at the given revelations, it's crucial to live vigilant and now not get manipulated at the palms of a psychopath unknowingly. Thereby, we need to discover ways to spot a person with narcissistic inclinations to keep away from toxicity in our lives while teaching ourselves the way to cope with psychopaths, on the equal time as wished.

four.1 - HOW TO SPOT A PSYCHOPATH

Scientists normally perform mind scans to analyze the emotional and morality scale for detecting capability psychopaths. However, because you could't have that desire at your disposal when meeting each exceptional man or woman on your existence, you have to revert to precise strategies to estimate whether or now not you're dealing with a real-existence psychopath.

After reviewing a few precise latest studies completed on the language of psychopaths, it came to our records that most of them can be detected based totally mostly on the way they hold a communique and behave. While the variations are extra often than now not diffused, we would notice them inadvertently, considering that our defenses are within the main already up on the identical time as meeting with strangers.

Here are ten vast verbal exchange and behavioral patterns found through maximum psychopaths which you need to be seeking out for:

1- They Usually Think, and Therefore, Speak within the Past Tense

When speakme approximately the existing activities, maximum people commonly talk like, "I assume, I can, I am." However, even as psychopaths speak, they may be saying a few component inside the lines, "I idea, I need to, I changed into." That's due to the fact while everyday human beings speak approximately some thing that's taking place proper then, they're usually mentally present within the interim. On the contrary, psychopaths aren't emotionally related to the concept of what they should be announcing, which leads them to talk as though it's all inside the past.

Researchers finish that psychopaths will be predisposed to speak as though what they will be speakme approximately has already occurred because of their cognitively indifferent behavior. Moreover, it's a trait that you may relate to as well, as you can on occasion find your self doing the same component whilst you enjoy like some thing you're speaking about isn't always interesting to you. Think approximately the times you had to consciously take some time to stay within the 2nd and try remembering how you conversed with others then. We wager you'll relate to these occurrences as properly. However, inside the case of psychopaths, these are normal times in place of seldom ones.

2- They Know How to Charm a Crowd

You also can in no manner meet a extra charming character on your lifestyles than a psychopath. Of route, not every distinct fascinating person you meet must be a sociopathic narcissist. However, it's one function that need to not be overlooked while mixed with awesome tendencies that in shape a psychopath's persona.

Additionally, numerous researchers have mentioned that psychopaths normally study the humans round them to get the gist earlier than they attempt the usage of emotional and non secular phrases themselves. That's furthermore why psychopaths are typically the top notch at pronouncing the proper topics at the right time. They're hold close manipulators who've executed their homework higher than you could remember earlier than trying it out with others.

3- Their Body Language is Convincing, But Their Expressions Are Not

A psychopath is aware about a way to maintain their very personal close to pulling off an act. They apprehend how their body language can paintings in their want masterfully. So, they watch and studies from the excellent of the top notch. They even train themselves excessively on a manner to seize others' interest while saying the right subjects one craves to listen.

However, irrespective of how sturdy their interpersonal skills are, the only detail that they might't control to supply out compellingly is their facial functions. While words can lie to the high-quality dad and mom, numerous humans usually usually tend to healthy words with expressions as nicely. Today's increasingly more decepetive worldwide has taught masses parents to glimpse inside the unique individual's eyes and notice the emotions swirling in them earlier than believing in some factor. If that's the case with you, this thoughts-set might paintings to your decide on on the equal time as speakme to a capability psychopath.

4- They Speak Softly

Studies display that maximum psychopaths determine on to talk in a relaxed, managed, and easy way in comparison to their aggressive personalities. They suppose that crafting a chilled demeanor will help them connect to others greater quick whilst being misinterpreted as a rational person.

However, it's also properly really worth noticing that their smooth tone stays pretty independent throughout the verbal exchange in most of the instances. While you might imagine in their speakme mannerism as uniquely touchy, you can additionally't forget about the lacking zest and enthusiasm of their voice that ordinary humans commonly have. Even inside the event that they get themselves to sound obsessed on some aspect, you could't assist but see that there's no trace of emotional extension within the returned in their terms. Again, it's a subtle trait however one that might display beneficial to you at times.

5- It's in Their Nature to Stir Up a Chaos

Just because psychopaths show off a peaceful demeanor doesn't advise they're able to't create a chaotic mess out of any situation. In reality, they love to play harmless on the equal time as blaming others for their reactions. In extraordinary terms, a psychopath works tough to provoke you in some manner. Then, at the equal time as you legitimately react, they act as if you're being hypersensitive. They may also moreover even act boastful, pronouncing things like, "I can't communicate to you about a few thing whilst you hold flipping out!"

That's essentially the forestall goal of a psychopath - to make you keep in mind that they may be the calm, rational ones, even as you're the overly sensitive nutcase. It ultimately diminishes your credibility now not truly in one-of-a-kind's eyes however for you as properly. You could in all likelihood encounter such psychopaths on your place of job or perhaps whilst you're supposedly building a courting with one unknowingly.

6- Turning People Against Each Other is Their Speciality

As an extension of the closing factor we mentioned, psychopaths exit in their way to expose people in competition to every other, even while you don't understand it. Their manner of 'gossiping' is virtually no longer like ordinary people, as they may be willing to pop out due to the fact the logical ones who may additionally need to do no wrong. However, their innocently toxic phrases do absolutely as tremendous of a project for them, if now not better.

Simply located, psychopaths pick the use of 'awful me' tales and faux issues to modify your notion of any other man or woman. Even when you have no opinion through any manner approximately the person they're speakme about, their come-up testimonies will activate you to create one although.

7- They Mostly Speak in Terms of Facts

Psychopaths with a higher strain for committing crimes are more likely to speak in phrases of statistics, despite the fact that they're speakme about hurting someone. For instance, serial killers don't usually shield their moves with the useful resource of developing with reminiscences. Contrarily, they outline the situation as a reality, saying such things as, "I needed to train him a lesson." It is as easy as that for them. Their actions are based on a motive, and they don't care how that could have an impact on the humans round them.

eight- They Use Filler Words More Often

We all use filler phrases, simply so's no longer a big deal. However, even as everyday humans use the terms like "uh" and "um," it's usually to avoid awkward silences or fill in the gaps at the identical time as speaking approximately a touchy problem be counted with hesitation. While it's now not constantly taken into consideration an tremendous signal to pick filler terms in particular settings, it's natural for us to use them every now and then.

However, psychopaths don't normally use filler terms out of necessity. They can't care tons much less about filling inside the silences, and it's hardly ever of their interpersonal dispositions to hesitate earlier than talking their mind. So, specially, they quality use filler phrases, because it's what they see other people doing. Their efforts to mixture in the society push them to behave like others in choice to appearing insanely non-being concerned. But research show that maximum psychopaths, even as they don't even recognise it themselves, do it a long manner more regularly than a median individual.

nine- They Are Phenomenal Storytellers

All psychopaths are brilliant storytellers. While they're someone's victim in plenty in their mock-up recollections, the majority of their stories are created to colour them because the shining heroes. A psychopath can also inform tall memories of valor. They also can furthermore tell you that they rescued a kitten from a building on hearth or had been the simplest one to upward thrust as much as their control at their very last system. However, all their rich memories are designed to stir up feelings that advantage others' do not forget.

If you be aware someone deliberately looking for to make you revel in like they may be the fine beings inside the global, it's higher to be extra stable in preference to sorry. Because once in a while in existence, on the identical time as it looks like some thing is simply too right to be true, it honestly is.

10- In the End, It's All About Their Needs

Feeling empathy for others is an alien idea to psychopaths. Moreover, even if there's a probable risk of having stuck in a lie or a deceiving motion, they appear unconcerned with the consequences. After spending only a few minutes speakme with them, you may realise that most of their conversations revolve spherical themselves. They could probably even be caught in a difficult state of affairs, but all they will don't forget can be associated with their needs and choices.

For instance, even supposing a psychopath confesses to a homicide, maximum in their time is spent speakme approximately such things as what they ate for lunch that day and what they was hoping to advantage from their moves. It's all about exciting their dreams on the price of numerous humans's intellectual, emotional, and bodily fitness.

4.2 - HOW TO DEAL WITH PSYCHOPATHS

There are times whilst we aren't cautious sufficient, or at the equal time as the psychopaths we've encountered are sadly too professional in concealing who they are. No count number huge range the purpose, whilst you discover your self strolling along a toxic man or woman or in a courting with one, you want to recognize a manner to deal with them to restrict the damage.

While most people assume they'd in no way probable meet a psychopath in lifestyles, the truth is that an entire lot of humans experience exactly the equal way earlier than they cave in the darkish hole. At instances like this, you have to recognize what's the fine approach to deal with the given state of affairs without stirring up any negativity, as that'll great turn out to be hurting you in place of the narcissistic psychopaths.

Here are seven subjects that professionals propose you can do to cope with manipulative humans with slight psychopathic dispositions:

1- Don't Engage with Them At All, If Possible

We are aware about it's now not as easy as announcing the magic word and breaking your reference to them. But that's your first preference except. For example, the immediate you apprehend you're in a relationship with a psychopath, you have got the choice to interrupt it off with them in location of gambling their undertaking. It's exceptional to region up as a bargain distance amongst yourself and them as possible because of the truth you can't win with them ever. They're a protracted manner better at making you sense like now not some thing than you could ever consider. After all, most psychopaths are already doing the same difficulty again and again their whole existence.

On the contrary, whilst it's no longer viable now not to extract yourself from their existence, like managing a psychopath coworker, it is better not to pique their interest and withstand the temptation of competing with them. The greater you keep away from assignment banters with them, the a great deal less risk there'll be of you turning into a threat for them.

2- Swallow the Bitter Pill and Accept What They Really Are

You may also moreover do not forget that everybody has particular in them with the ability to be a higher character. While it's real to a degree, this logic wouldn't do you any appropriate inside the case of psychopaths. The superb rule for dealing with such human beings is to swallow the bitter tablet and be for the reason that some people haven't any ethical revel in, first of all.

You can't change how a psychopath thinks or acts. It's of their very personal arms to manipulate their impulses and make a distinction. Moreover, they take it as a project on the same time as a person confronts their way of processing precise mind, making their lifestyles a hell in flow returned.

3- Address Your Weaknesses As Well

Psychopaths are specialists in figuring out different humans's weaknesses, particularly when they revel in like they may be being targeted. That's why you want to address your shortcomings whilst you discover your self stuck with a psychopath. When you extensively identified your faults and art work on them discreetly, it leaves the psychopaths no alternative however to go away you alone, due to the truth there'd be nothing to make the most.

4- Pay Attention to What They Do, Not What They Say

All psychopaths are fascinating talkers and storytellers, it truely is why you want to make it a rule of thumb no longer to get inspired through absolutely everyone's phrases. Instead, it's generally on your first-rate interest to be privy to human beings's actions and behavior. However, it's additionally crucial to tell sincere mistakes from deceitful and toxic conduct.

Manipulation is the linchpin of unscrupulous behavior. You might not come upon a lie the number one time, wondering it is a false impression. The 2d time a person neglects their obligation may be them developing a grave mistake. However, 3 extreme lies or deceitful moves in a row mean you're managing a pathological liar and a particular exploiter.

5- Keep Your Emotions in Check and Don't Get Intimidated

It's critical to keep your calm and no longer get intimidated by using others with toxic dispositions. Losing your temper or often getting annoyed with others gives a psychopath extra energy over you, because it makes you appear to be an clean purpose.

Once a psychopath realizes how reachable it's far for them to manipulate your feelings, they maintain to stand over you and get you to back off. In such times, recognition your floor is vital for supplying yourself as a person not to be messed with.

6- Don't Let Them Stamp Out Your Reputation

Psychopaths have a knack for recruiting "buddies in the higher control" to offer them cowl whilst rumors start escalating approximately their shady conduct. Moreover, the identical assets make it much less complicated for them to unfold lies and disinformation approximately in fact every person moving into their manner or posing a hazard.

To avoid being one of the humans they may ruin, you want to begin from scratch and gather your very very personal reputation. When you aren't visible as a complainer, making an investment your power and building sincere relationships give you an component within the worst of instances. Moreover, whilst you find out your confidants telling you that the person you're going for walks or in a courting with isn't specific for you, you may need to concentrate carefully to their motives in preference to protective others.

7- Propose Win-Win Agreements, If Need Be

Manipulation and aggression are of psychopaths' great tendencies. They want to win in each component of lifestyles, although they ought to take extreme steps to reap this. That's why it's miles excellent to research the paintings of imparting win-win conditions to them at the same time as you discover them taking walks along you.

When you're making it less complicated for your self and them to paintings collectively, there may be fewer possibilities of kicking off a competition which you want no part of. While schooling this knowledge calls for creativity and a particular attitude from your facet, it's probably the quality tool to deal with a psychopath.

four.Three - THE FINAL VERDICT

On the one hand, there are psychopaths with zero empathy and regret. However, alternatively, there are people with Williams Syndrome. These people have an excessive amount of integrated compassion of their nature, as they bear in mind and take delivery of as actual with in all of us. Most folks fall into a category that's positioned someplace in amongst.

The point of declaring that is to honestly receive the notion that we are able to come upon all sorts of people in lifestyles. The most effective manner to defend ourselves on the same time as preserving sane isn't to permit a horrific existence experience overrun our recall from the entire community. Instead, the outstanding way to cope with the abnormalities of existence is to strike a stability amongst both aspects and stop scrutinizing the area in black and white. We need to discover ways to have a look at our activities first after which act consequently.

BREAKING THE PERNICIOUS CHAIN OF PSYCHOPATHY

W

e are dedicating the closing economic disaster to speak approximately the importance of breaking this bad cycle of psychopathy. It is essential to realize that most psychopaths don't surely rework their character in a single day upon becoming adults. In fact, they're usually great from an early age.

It is immoderate time someone factors out that almost all of people dwelling in our society neglect about the smooth signs and symptoms in a toddler showing worrisome signs and symptoms, wondering it's terrific 'a segment.' When in reality, that's genuinely the begin of a massive catastrophe. We need to experience the duty as human beings to make a contribution to our society and now not forsake any development of capability pathological symptoms.

By following the preventive measures, we are capable of smash or, at the least, slow down this pernicious chain in advance than it receives underway. Once we perform our obligation as a responsible citizen in area of being a negligent figure, aunt, uncle, or passerby, it's pretty probable we're able to turn this society proper proper right into a better community.

In smooth terms, it's miles critical to educate our youngsters approximately psychopathy, bringing it to mild how we're able to stray our extra youthful generation away from such intensive and toxic behaviors.